World Peace

By

Burl Minnis

Copyright

Copyright © 2025 Burl Minnis

Published by

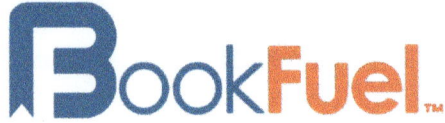

"Those who can make you believe absurdities can make you commit atrocities".

– Voltaire.

Table of Content

Part I
The Age of the Swindle

Chapter 1: Understanding the Swindle

Summary: The Problem before Us

This is going to be fun. It is, after all, world peace. And, it certainly has been for me, so far. Thirty-five days after publication of this work, it will be your turn to chime in. Certainly, you can feel free to do so, if you like, any time before then; I just figured I'd give you time to read this. Nonetheless, that global authority on this matter, that you'll be sending your submissions to, should you choose to contribute your voice to the majority, have already seen this work, know that this book is coming, and are, now, expecting your correspondences.

https://otplink.icc-cpi.int

The Prosecutors Office of the International Criminal Court (POICC) has policies for submission, and those need to be followed as prescribed on their website. But they have known about this solution for world peace since 2012, and under Article 15 of the Rome Statute, they have made provisions to hear our voices on this matter. (So, tell everyone you know about this, too). And, yes; that means that you're only the second to know about world peace, and the "powers that be" worldwide, were the first. Sorry it took me so long to get here. But you, the humans reading this, right now, are the only ones that matter. So, chime in, and tell all your friends to do the same.

I'm just the messenger, here, too. Everyone else said this stuff; not me. I'm just telling you what they said. But turn to my bibliography, and you'll get to see who said what about all of this, and when they said it. I'm not sure how such a

WORLD PEACE

fundamental solution was missed for all these millennia; that's outside the purview of this work. Those people in my bibliography simply missed it so, naturally, we missed it, too, as their audience. Nothing nefarious, no maniacal intent, no great plan of secrecy; they just never saw it, so we never got it. Fortunately, the majority of humans on the planet got it, and this then is the message.

You may know them as the "silent majority", of common mind and few words. Not silent because they have nothing to say, but rather that they say nothing. They are the live and let live, types, or the mind your manners and you'll keep your friends, group, or the when in Rome do as the Romans do, crowd. You probably know them if you're not one of the majority, yourself. Like, if you find yourself yawning through this work, thinking to yourself, "yeah, kid; tell me something I don't know", well, you're probably in majority. Regardless, I impart no wisdom upon you that you didn't already possess.

Not to worry, though, I lay the majority voice out for you in the chapters that follow, quite thoroughly. And, no one needs to die for world peace. It's far too simple, direct, and instantaneous a solution to get all indignant about, and nothing changes, in any way, for humans. So, you might as well enjoy it, too.

The vast majority of human misery does not stem from blind fate, natural disasters, or even the malice of individuals acting alone. Instead, it arises from a single system—a complex, construct of organized, and/or institutionalized ideology, upon collective fiction being imposed on reality, and sustained through the willful suspension of disbelief in favor of the rules, or tools, or codes of law that make playing along with the fiction seem real. Think political ideology.

WORLD PEACE

Think monetary economy ideology (commonly agreed-upon value) These ideologies, have become so deeply integrated into the fabric of daily life that we mistake their operation and effects for natural laws or realities themselves. Instead, they have proven to be the system of all human misery.

It began for Man as long as 300,000 years ago with the natural human appreciation for value. While such a notion might seem innocuous enough. that concept then evolved in the minds of Man, just as Man adapted to planetary evolution, culminating 13,000 years ago with the "Age of the Swindle". This period in human development, then, saw "the great burn", necessitating the height of human imagination and resiliency be brought to bear to overcome the latest climatic event to befall us. And it worked. But we never turned it off after it saved us. And, it has been our system of all human misery, as a species, ever since.

The conation that ideology could influence reality using a universal translation tool we call money became a conative toxin in the minds of Man ever since. Think of it as the first industrial accident of Man—a massive deception of organized, and/or institutionalized ideology that has entrapped humanity for millennia in the system of all human misery, and whose unraveling is essential for achieving any substantively lasting peace.

The good news is that every system has a keystone, which once removed, causes change in the system. In this case of the system of all human misery, the system changes to become more amenable for all life on Earth. Which, will be important for those last 1,000 years we have left, as a species. The system of all human misery has brought about our extinction 150 years ago, and when we go, we are taking 97% of life with us.

WORLD PEACE

The only problem Man has ever faced for 13,000 years since the Age of the Swindle began, has been money. Everything else that we might hold in vile disdain and point fingers at and cast blame on as our problems are but symptoms of our single problem. It's the keystone in the system of all human misery, in fact. Which, once removed, makes life more amenable. Fort all living things. But nothing changes in the way we do anything. Our receipts just read 0.00. World peace is only two words: abolish money. The process of execution is only six: set all general ledgers to zero. Then, just pick a day and walk away. And, nothing changes in the way we, as a species, do anything, except that money no longer stands in the way of human rights, and/or birthrights.

Now, read on and find out why that is your irrefutable, undeniable, and unabashed solution for world peace. And then, contribute your voice, and tell all your friends to do the same. We'll all come in for the big win, together, and no one needs to die for world peace. After 12 years, already, that this work has been assessed and reviewed on the world stage, the POICC is really just waiting on you. It actually is that simple.

The Messenger

In this work, I do not claim originality for the ideas presented; I am but a messenger, a conduit through which an ancient yet enduring reality is being conveyed by the majority of reasonable, rational human actors the world over. I don't care why it has to be me. No one picked me. The majority are of common mind and few words. The "silent majority", as it were. The world over.

So, I'm just not waiting on them. We're extinct now, as a species, and we don't have long left. We have to snap out of

WORLD PEACE

it, now, and come in for the big win together. There's a lot of work to do. You cannot have trash without money, and you cannot have war without politics. We need to snap out of that first industrial accident of Man, that conative toxin and its related mental malady because that last 3% of all life in the universe to survive us, will need a leg up from the toxicity of the human footprint. So, this is just what the majority say.

The evidence for the existence of our system of all human misery is visible everywhere, embedded in history, in social structures, in recurring patterns of conflict and suffering. It is a reality that has been known, articulated, and rediscovered countless times over the centuries by thinkers, philosophers, activists, and observers across cultures and epochs.

What is now required is not new knowledge or novel theory. Our libraries and archives are filled with studies, analyses, empirical data, and philosophical insights that reveal the mechanisms and consequences of the ideological fictions of money, politics, power, and celebrity. And, that's in spite of all the losses in trustworthy knowledge suffered by our species to the ravages of theology, or war, or antiquity. The foundational concepts for the Age of the Swindle have been illuminated repeatedly, from the warnings of Enlightenment thinkers like Voltaire to the critiques of modern social scientists (Szasz, 1973; Zmigrod, 2021).

I'll get into the solution more as you read on, but for now, our challenge today is fundamentally one of courage and collective will—the courage to see beyond deeply ingrained illusions, to confront uncomfortable realities, and to act decisively in the face of systemic inertia and vested interests. I cannot obligate you on this. That would constitute involuntary slavery. Humans cannot obligate humans. Humans obligate themselves. So, I have to ask you. I'll impart upon you no wisdom with this work that you didn't already possess, but I will make the reality of all you know very clear. The facts of the matter, as it were, absent any ideology story. Trustworthy knowledge alone, however, cannot free us; action built upon conviction and awareness is indispensable. It will, in fact, require that you contribute your voice to the POICC in order to achieve world peace, but nothing more. So, make sure you tell all your friends. The more the merrier. And the sooner the better.

This book is therefore not a work of fiction or escapist idealism, but a firm call to grasp reality as it is—free from the myths and ideological distortions that masquerade as truth. Recognizing the Age of the Swindle for what it is means acknowledging how deeply we have been enmeshed in belief systems that distort our perception of what is possible, what is just, and what is natural. So, when you see the distortions for yourself by the end of this work, let the POICC know, and we are on our way to finally fixing all of them, all at once, for the rest of our time.

By illuminating this deception, this work is an invitation to choose a different path—one that transcends the divisive and destructive fictions of the money and the politics ideology system of all human misery, and embrace cooperation, peace, and shared humanity. It's how our species was so successful for over 200,000 years, already, right up to 13,000 years ago. We're just fixing that industrial accident. Advocate for world peace through your voiced contribution to the POICC. And, no one needs to die for world peace. We just all come in for the big win, together.

Burl Minnis

WORLD PEACE

The path forward demands collective responsibility. Each individual has the power to break the cycle by refusing to endorse or participate in the fictional systems that perpetuate misery. Such refusal is not passive resignation but a powerful form of resistance and reclamation of free will. Set all general ledgers to zero, and walk away. We just need to pick a day. Monetary economy ideology was the first. The tool supporting the fiction was money. It represents the keystone in the system of all human misery, which once removed results in a more amenable system. In our case, for all life on Earth. And nothing changes. Everything we do today with money, we'll do exactly the same way tomorrow without money. It's not like we aren't already making it today, anyway, and money doesn't even enter into those conversations until after the fact as it is. Everyone works first and gets paid later. Well, keep the paycheck, I got no debts, I got no bills. And if I want something, I'll go get it. My receipt will just say 0.00. I'll get into it more as you read on, but its everything we have today in this scenario, and really that easy to achieve world peace. But you'll need to know why, (if you don't already) so I'll drone on.

The history of human civilization shows that systems founded on fictions can endure only as long as we collectively uphold them. When enough people see through the illusion and withdraw their consent, systemic change—peaceful and transformative—becomes inevitable. The keystone in the system of all human misery is money; the only problem Man has ever faced since the Age of the Swindle, ideology itself, began. And, the system can be dismantled without violence, through shared awareness and unified action (Estes et al., 2016).

The messenger role is both a responsibility and a privilege: to convey these facts without embellishment or distortion, to arm readers with trustworthy knowledge, and to inspire courage. The potential for world peace lies not in the invention of new ideas but in the rediscovery and re-embodiment of facts long known.

This book is a call to reality—a summons to see the world unflinchingly, to understand the roots of human suffering, and to participate in the collective decision to end the Age of the Swindle. World peace is the beginning of a new chapter, where acknowledging reality becomes the foundation for creating a future of genuine lasting peace and real human prosperity.

The Path Forward

As we venture deeper into this work, the forthcoming chapters are designed to systematically unpack the complex layers behind the Age of the Swindle—the grand ideological illusion that has entrapped humanity and fueled much of its persistent suffering in the system of all human misery. At the risk of seeming redundant, each chapter will provide a standalone exposition, carefully structured so that readers may approach them in any order according to their interest or urgency. This modular approach respects the diverse backgrounds and priorities of readers, encouraging a personalized journey through the evidence, the arguments, and most importantly, the ever-obvious solution.

Throughout these chapters, you will be guided through a rich bibliography—an essential compass pointing to the foundational sources, thinkers, and research that have shaped, challenged, and confirmed the ideas presented here. This is what everyone else is already telling you about a host of subjects. Engaging with this body of work is a vital part of the process; it encourages you not only to absorb but to critically examine the claims made, to explore alternate perspectives, and to question deeply the assumptions that underpin the systems we live within (Szasz, 1973; Zmigrod, 2021; Estes et al., 2016).

Reading widely and questioning rigorously are active intellectual practices that nurture the discernment required to disentangle the layers of ideology and fiction from empirical reality. This invitation to scholarship is not a call for passive reception but for an interactive dialogue—between author, text, and reader—allowing individual and collective insights to emerge. Moreover, you are encouraged to bring your own lived experiences, observations, and reflections into this discourse. The collective understanding and effort towards world peace will be richer and more resilient when diverse voices and perspectives contribute to the POICC.

As the work progresses towards its conclusion, you will face a profound invitation: to make a conscious choice regarding the path of humanity. This is not merely an academic exercise or philosophical option, but a decisive moment of practical agency. Your contribution will be remembered by all who succeed us for the rest of our time. The power to end the Age of the Swindle resides not solely in the hands of elite decision-makers or isolated activists or some brilliance in our species as yet to be born; it belongs to every individual who recognizes the facts and is willing to act upon them. Then, advocate for this solution with the majority and come on in for the big win.

The fate of humanity—whether we continue down the path of systemic misery or pivot toward peace and flourishing— depends fundamentally on this collective decision. The system of all human misery ends when we decide it ends— a succinct yet powerful declaration that spotlights the crucial role of human volition. By withdrawing belief, consent, and participation in the ideological systems of money, and politics, we dissolve the very foundations of the system of all human misery without the need for violence or upheaval (Estes et al., 2016).

This decision entails embracing reality, with all its challenges and potentials, rather than clinging to comforting fictions that lead only to devastation. Even corporations record a net-net of zero in the black, so everything goes on just fine. It means reclaiming our shared humanity, reviving timeless virtues, and committing to a future where world peace is not an abstract ideal but an everyday lived condition.

The chapters to come are thus both diagnostic and prescriptive. They will show how entrenched the Age of the Swindle is, using rigorous historical, economic, and social analysis, but equally they will illuminate paths for dismantling the system of all human misery through conscious, collective action rooted in empirical understanding and resolve.

You are encouraged to view this book not as the final word, but as a catalyst—for learning, dialogue, and, ultimately, action. The transformation it calls for is both urgent and deeply hopeful: to move beyond a world dominated by fictions toward one grounded in reality, justice, and genuine lasting peace.

The Role and Nature of the Swindle

To grasp the Age of the Swindle fully, it is crucial to recognize that it is neither a discrete event nor a conspiracy orchestrated by a hidden cabal. It is, instead, a long and

WORLD PEACE

ongoing process—an entrapping of humanity within a maze of its own collective beliefs, sustained through shared acceptance of constructed fictions. The Age of the Swindle manifests through the systematic elevation of ideology over actual reality. It is the system of all human misery, and every system has its keystone. I'll get into it all more as you read on, but for now, that process of elevating fiction over fact is exclusively responsible for all crimes against humanity and war crimes since the practice began.

Ideology, by its very nature, is a set of normative ideas about how the world ought to be rather than descriptive truths about how the world actually is (Zmigrod, 2021). When such prescriptive ideas are mistaken for, or imposed as, natural facts—when they become rigidly institutionalized and elicit unquestioning allegiance—the result is systemic injustice, conflict, and widespread suffering. The system of all human misery. And the only problem Man has ever faced since its inception is the keystone for that system.

Prominent among these constructed fictions are money and politics. Money is fundamentally a symbolic construct—a system of promises, a shared belief in value that has no intrinsic physical guarantee but relies entirely on collective trust and agreement through the use of a tool. Similarly, political entities such as ideological parties, corporations, and public sector markets, et al. are not natural phenomena but social inventions—complex artifacts of collective imagination that have been granted agency and power by either code of law or various spurious rules, as if they were living beings.

We have anthropomorphized these abstractions (Seltzer, 2012), imbuing institutions and economic systems with rights and powers that properly belong only to living individuals. This inversion has stifled essential human virtues—honor, nobility, wisdom, and imagination—while entrenching systemic oppression.

See Figure 1 in the appendix section for the timeframe that The Age of the Swindle covers

Historical and Structural Origins

Tracing the Swindle's origins reveals a long evolution from ancient myth-making to modern institutionalized ideology. Human societies have always used stories to create shared understandings, bind groups together, and justify hierarchies and power structures. These narratives hardened over time into rigid ideologies embedded within religions, kingdoms, empires, and eventually sovereign nation-states (Szasz, 1973).

You can see Figure 1 for a comprehensive timeline, but the advent of money as a universal medium of exchange marked a pivotal moment in this history. Money is essentially a symbolic promise, a shared belief in value untethered from the direct utility of an item or service. Today, it's all "implied wealth", today, and faith-based market economies, and money even changes its value by the nanosecond, so there's no agreed-upon anything, commonly or otherwise, in order to gage value. We just make it up day-to-day. And, every time it fails—which is, historically, every few decades—every time we experience yet another global economic cascade failure, we murder millions. That constitutes a crime against humanity since everyone must do the economy ideology. And, there's no trash, or greed, without it.

Originally devised to facilitate our survival, as a species, during critical existential threats—such as "the great burn"

WORLD PEACE

extinction-level event about 13,000 years ago—monetary economy introduced a new psychological dimension to humanity's relations: ideology.

This form of commonly agreed-upon value, then, became the first ideology of Man, and acts as a conative toxin repressing human potential. In addition, its tool of money introduced a new mental malady previously unknown to Man, as well, which we commonly experience as greed. Nothing else in the universe inspires greed in Man besides money, and nothing good ever came from greed.

This greed, absent in natural ecosystems and pre-ideological human communities, acts as an exacerbator for other mental maladies already in human experience such as egomania from power and narcissism from celebrity. Greed only makes all these worse.

Politics emerged around 8,000 years ago, formalizing governance and societal divisions. Its survival depends fundamentally on creating and maintaining divisions—the "us versus them" mentality—that inherently generate conflict and ensure continuous warfare. Anthropological evidence suggests no wars occurred before the institutionalization of politics, confirming that war is a political invention—a fiction imposed upon humanity for control and exploitation.

But the monetary economy ideology has its divisiveness, too. Ideology of every type and kind require divisiveness, in fact, or they cannot persist. So, there are always the "haves" and "have nots" in monetary economy ideology, as well. And, as long as we have to pay for our human rights, and/or birthrights, we are all also enslaved by the monetary economy ideology which constitutes crimes against humanity, if not human rights violations. Self-preservation (healthcare) and self-defense (legal representation) are human rights. We don't pay for those. And, intriguingly, they are the only two professions of Man that do get paid first, and work later. Lawyers by retainer and healthcare by insurance premiums.

This practice of elevating fiction over reality became the Age of the Swindle, marked by the system of all human misery. It is the systemic conjunction of money and politics, each reinforcing the other's fictions and producing a framework of control and misery couched as "normalcy". While only 40% of humans on the planet do the politics ideology in any way, everyone is enslaved to the monetary economy ideology.

After 13,000 years of trying, we haven't been able to buy our ways out of this system of all human misery, either, nor has politics ever solved anything during all of its time as a misery in human experience. Or we would be at peace, already. World peace will, quite literally, require every penny on the planet for all of time, all at once. It is the keystone.

The Way Forward: Ending the Swindle

The Age of the Swindle is neither designed by malice nor sustained solely by power-hungry elites. Instead, all humans participate in it, whether knowingly or not, acting as willing or unwitting enablers of the system.

Despite its enormous power, the system of all human misery is fragile at its core because it depends entirely on collective belief. Its keystone is the tool itself, used to make the first ideology seem real., whose removal precipitates systemic

WORLD PEACE

collapse and opens the possibility for genuine peace (Estes et al., 2016).

This collapse need not be violent or traumatic. Rather, it can occur if humanity collectively chooses to stop believing in money and politics as realities—to "set all general ledgers to zero"—and thereby walk away from the fictions that sustain human misery. And nothing changes in the way Man does anything. Nobody gets paid first, for instance. We all work first, everywhere, and get paid later. Well, the needful thing is already done. Keep the paycheck. I got no debts, no bills; what would I do with it? And humans are once again free from their first breaths.

Abolishing money clears the path to:

- Restoring natural human reason and rationale.
- Ending war, hunger, inequality, and trash.
- Enabling free will free from greed and divisiveness.
- Reclaiming trustworthy knowledge, value, and virtue as the drivers of social organization.
- Not to mention equity, sustainability, nobility, honor, wisdom, imagination, et al., but you can read on to see the list is quite long.

World peace is thus a practical outcome, contingent upon an awakening to the reality about the system of all human misery and the courage to abandon it. And, yes, of course; letting the POICC know about your decision, too. They will advise the UN of the majority mind on this matter, the UN will pick a date, and poof; world peace. The emergency broadcasting mechanisms of everywhere will ensure timely alert for everyone everywhere, so no big deal. We have everything we need except your voice.

Understanding the Age of the Swindle emerges as the essential first step toward ending it. The nonliving entity constructs we have built —money, politics, corporations, countries—are neither natural nor inevitable. They are the products of collective human storytelling, of ideological fictions that govern our behavior and impose misery. While individually practiced, ideology is fine to believe, or trust. But you cannot run a planet by it. Anytime ideology is organized or institutionalized into those nonliving entity constructs we've built for ourselves; suffering begins. And, that's suffering of all life. Ending the Swindle is not a utopian fantasy but grounded in empirical observation, historical evidence, and sound reasoning. It requires recognizing the constructed nature of these systems and choosing to disengage. The power that system of all human misery holds over us dissolves the moment we reject its narratives. The Age of the Swindle can end, making way for a new era—one founded on reality, peace, and the flourishing of human potential.

The Age of the Swindle

The Core Argument

To understand the systemic swindle of organized, and/or institutionalized, ideology, it is essential to first appreciate its vast scope and subtle nature. The Age of the Swindle is not a singular event occurring at a fixed point in history, nor is it the outcome of a secretive cabal manipulating humanity from behind the scenes. Rather, it is a prolonged, systemic entrapment of humanity within a shared fiction of its own creation marked by that organized, and/or institutionalized ideological system of all human misery. It manifests as a process whereby societies, economies, and governments are founded and sustained by collective belief in things that have no concrete, empirical reality, and no hope of solving anything. One cannot throw fiction at reality and expect a positive outcome.

At its essence, the system of all human misery is the elevation of ideology above reality. Ideology—whether religious, economic, political, or cultural—is by definition a set of prescriptive ideas about how the world ought to be, rather than descriptive truths about how the world actually is (Zmigrod, 2021). When these ideologies are mistaken for reality, or are imposed rigidly as natural laws rather than human-made constructs, they generate suffering on a massive and systemic scale.

Consider the example of money—a widely accepted social institution that drives human economies and lives. Money, in reality, is not a tangible object of inherent value but a fictional construct, a symbolic certificate of trust or promissory note that operates solely because large groups of people agree to treat it as valuable. Similarly, corporations, countries, and private sector markets are social inventions— conceptual entities created to organize human activity, but not existing as natural or living things.

Consider the practice of voting. A privilege, not a right. Acts do have rights any more than things do. Only living entities have rights, and humans are free from their first breaths. They need not do anything to ensure that. The vote, then, is electing to subjugate oneself to another. The exact opposite of freedom. But institutionalized politics cannot persist unless citizens remain confused about civics, and what constitutes a majority. You can see Figure 2 in the appendix for more on this from the US, at least. But statistics works, so its universal among our species. So saith the majority.

Yet, society has come to anthropomorphize these institutions (Seltzer, 2012), ascribing them agency, rights, and powers traditionally reserved for living beings. This fundamental confusion—the substitution of social fiction for reality— suppresses essential human qualities like virtue, honor, nobility, imagination, and wisdom, because these intangible fictions demand obedience, conformity, and sacrifice.

Thus, the Age of the Swindle is the replacement of reality with ideology, and the profound misery that inevitably follows from this substitution.

The Origins of the Swindle

The question arises: how did humanity come to live within this Age of the Swindle? The story is as ancient as civilization itself.

From the dawn of human social life, our ancestors created stories—narratives used to explain natural phenomena, to forge communal identity, and to justify hierarchical power structures. Mostly for personal amusement, initially, the suspension of disbelief required for such stories became mutually appreciated entertainment. This practice of suspending disbelief, of pretend along collectively, allowed these early stories to evolve into myths, which then hardened into ideologies. Over centuries and millennia, these ideologies became legalized institutions—religions, kingdoms, empires—and, eventually, modern nation-states (Szasz, 1973). The introduction and rise of money marked a transformative moment in this history. Monetary economy ideology is the first foray of Man into institutionalized ideology. Money is the universal translation tool for the commonly agreed-upon value within that type of institutionalized ideology. Money is essentially a promise

WORLD PEACE

and symbol, a shared collective belief in value without inherent worth. It is not a physical thing but an agreed-upon idea. Despite this abstraction, over the centuries, humans have come to treat money as the most real and consequential "thing" in the world, assigning it interpretative priority even over human life itself. Hence, the first industrial accident of Man, a conative toxin that murders millions each time it fails, the practice of which is responsible for a preponderance of crimes against humanity, human rights violations, and/or war crimes, and the prolonged exposure to money motives creates the mental malady of greed as an exacerbator for repression of human virtue.

Humans do diplomacy, as do many other organisms regardless of their social or isolationist inclinations as species'. We mind our manners, we keep our friends, for instance. When in Rome, we do as the Romans do, and all that. The politics ideology was the first creation from the Age of the Swindle. Politics emerged from the diplomacy framework to serve as a mechanism for the management and organization of these fictions for the purpose of pursuing and acquiring money. It is the art of persuading people to believe one story over another, to rally around symbols, flags, identities, and ideologies that exist only because people agree to those beliefs. Politics, thus, perpetuates the Age of the Swindle by institutionalizing conflict and division and inequity, and all just to maintain power. Crucially, while some individuals benefit materially from sustaining the system of all human misery, it is collective participation by all of us, which fuels and upholds that system.

I'll say it again since it's important to remember; no ideology ever did anything, solved anything, benefited humans, in any way, or we wouldn't, still, have human misery after eight thousand years of trying to make the politics ideology work.

WORLD PEACE

Ideology only ever takes countries to war, politically, and/or economically. Illustrated in Figure 2, is the voter turnout for the United States in the 2020 presidential election. It is the table A-10, taken from the US Census Bureau website, and the link is, also, included in the Bibliography. Interestingly enough, the table A-10 on today's US Census website does not have the header information contained in Figure 2 (I added the total citizen population, and the yellow highlighted totals, rows, and the projected column for 2024 for convenience. There is, also, a link in Figure 2 for today's US Census version for ease of comparison).

The absence of the totals in today's US Census table A-10, may, or may not, be to intentionally obscure from the public the fact that only forty percent of citizens participate in voting, at all. But such is the case; only the minority does politics.

Absent, as well, are the total numbers of citizens who register as ideologues, simply for the purpose of registering for their civic responsibilities to do jury duty. In the US, at least, jury duty is tied directly to voter registration, and there is no other option to do jury duty for a US citizen except to register as a voter. Yet, thirteen and a half million citizens, consistently, will never cast a ballot. They just want to do jury duty. There are, also, two million children in the total US citizen numbers, who don't get representation, so they remain free from their first breaths, too. While all parents have an interest in their children's wellbeing, there is no voting by proxy, so parents vote in their own self-interest. It's why voting works. Further, the US has almost two million felons, who don't get the privilege of voting. They are, still, however, citizens, and, as such, members of the majority. But total population numbers are available elsewhere on the US Census website, so those numbers will need to be cobbled-together. The table in Figure 2 was taken in June of 2023, and all table A-10 data from the US Census, today, will obfuscate through omission that which is being presented in Figure 2, here, which, by extension, allows the politics ideology fiction to appear as if it is reality; as if politics is germane.

It should be noted, however, that it is not the job of the US Census Bureau to police voting, nor voter turnout data. They are, merely, the repository for such data, and their website is where that data is presented. Nonetheless, it is the bureaucracy that, actually, runs the country, and the majority citizens have elected to put the bureaucracy in charge, and not to fill those five hundred and nineteen thousand, eight hundred and sixty-two seats with any elected officials, at the local, state, and federal, levels of government, countrywide, across the executive, legislative, and judiciary, branches. And, that's been for 250 years in the US, at least. Political parties have merely obstructed majority rule, obfuscated the will of the citizens, and put people in those seats anyway. But, in all fairness, it is still possible for anyone to cobble-together the data necessary to construct the table information contained in Figure 2 from today's US Census website, provided the researcher knows that an omission exists. So, it is entirely possible that any obfuscation is coincidental. Yet, still, warrants investigation, or at least in-depth factchecking.

The Consequences of the Swindle

The consequences of this grand and persistent fiction are evident and tragic:

WORLD PEACE

Wars are waged over borders that exist only on maps, artificial lines drawn and respected not by natural forces but by political ideology.

Millions perish from starvation, not because there is an actual shortage of food globally, but because the fiction of money restricts access to necessary resources. Even human rights and/or birthright today have price tags.

Countless individuals live and die sacrificing their well-being for ideologies and concepts that have no genuine empirical basis, surrendering life to sustain a fiction. We even persist in forcing such nonsense to make sense without question as if life for any living entity is expected to be hard.

The system of all human misery is inherently self-perpetuating. It rewards compliance and punishes those who question or resist the prevailing fictions. Through this dynamic, absurdities become normalized, and what is truly rational or natural or intuitive becomes increasingly marginal or "unthinkable." As Voltaire famously warned, "Those who can make you believe absurdities can make you commit atrocities" (Szasz, 1973). The Age of the Swindle is the machinery turning belief into violence and atrocity by sustaining unfounded ideologies.

The System of All Human Misery

Crucially, the Age of the Swindle is not the deliberate product of evil individuals or secret conspirators. It is an emergent system, one that no single person or group designed but which everyone, consciously or subconsciously, participates in. This system can be aptly described as the system of all human misery and is comprised, exclusively, of the monetary economy ideology,

WORLD PEACE

as the first to emerge 13,000 years ago, and the politics ideology, emerging some 5,000 years later.

Global economic crises, which recur roughly every decade, destroy livelihoods not due to scarcity but due to the collapse of shared fictions in money and credit. Since humans no longer have the option of participation in this form of fiction, or not, because our human rights, and/or birthrights are not accessible without participation, such ideology constitutes involuntary servitude, and crimes against humanity

On average, every few weeks, conflicts erupt somewhere in the world, and people die in wars ignited by ideological disputes, further demonstrating how deeply this system is embedded in human conflict. Interestingly, only a minority of humans on the planet do this form of ideology. The majority of humans, everywhere, do not do politics. No ideology ever solved anything, and humans are advanced problem-solvers. Moreover, humans may be a species that cannot only kill each other, we can kill ourselves, as well; but we do not war. That is not a condition of the human existence. You have to have the politics ideology for that.

Show me any evidence of warfare in the archeological record prior to the formation of the first government 8,100 years ago. Show me any evidence there of homicide prior to 13,000 years ago. Now show me any evidence ever since. The system of all human misery kills on a massive scale— not out of explicit malice, but through the relentless and persistent insistence on divisiveness of its own ideological fictions. "them" and "us". "Haves" and "have nots". As a species, today, we perpetually force the nonsense of both ideologies in this system of all human misery to make sense. And, we actually feel bad, for instance, whenever the, "where are you going to get the money for that", or the "who do you think is going to pay for that", or the "do you know how much that will cost" nonsense allows children to starve, senselessly, and we are all sad. But fully understand because it is about money after all.

Well, if money is your problem, then get rid of your problem and just stop having any more problems. Easy. All human beings are, to some extent, slaves to this system. Some may even knowingly choose this subjugation, believing it brings security, prosperity, or meaning. Yet, in the final analysis, no one escapes the effects; everyone becomes a victim of the pervasive ideological illusion. The willful suspension of disbelief, by rule, and/or tool, and/or code of law. And, we are extinct, now, because of it.

The Illusion of Progress

Perhaps one of the most insidious deceptions created by the Age of the Swindle is the illusion that humanity is progressing—that reforms, innovations, and policies are gradually improving justice, prosperity, and peace.

However, this is itself a fiction.

In reality, the Age of the Swindle is adaptive and resilient. It absorbs every challenge, every critique, and every attempt at reform, over the millennia transforming these into additional layers of fiction and obfuscation that reinforce the power we bestow. The system is not broken in isolated parts that can be repaired here and there; rather, the fault lies in the foundational premise of mistaking fiction for reality.

Until this root error is confronted and resolved, all superficial improvements are ultimately temporary and illusory. The Age of the Swindle will endure and we'll

WORLD PEACE

continue to enjoy the system of all human misery. And, politics will perpetually insist on divisiveness among our species where absolutely none can exist among siblings in the last iteration from the family of Man.

The pursuit and acquisition of the almighty dollar has led to the infusion of ideology into corporate Charter, for instance, turning greed into an art form of avarice, but nothing close to progress. And, history is replete with captains of industry, and grand poohbahs of invention, and titans of whatever else, dragging humanity – often kicking and screaming about it – into modernity. And, all for a paycheck. Well, we're here, we can do whatever we need to do, now, so let's turn off the system of all human misery, and do these last 1,000 years we have left, at best, at peace.

We put a man on the Moon before putting wheels on luggage, so we don't have to go very far back in that history to see where unbridled avarice got us. Just look at computers, for example. Today, Man will never be any better than computers let us be, and we were already better before computers took over the job. Now, volatiles pollute the planet so we can have computers. You cannot have identity theft or piracy without computers. We, as a species, had to double our energy production just to have computers (and with A.I., humans need to commit to producing four times more than we need), and we are truly a paperless society, now, because every bit and byte, every 0 and 1 being turned back into paper would deforest the entire planet 18 times with 80% of human data still left irrecoverable. And, all for a paycheck.

It doesn't just have to be technological progress that gets called into question, though. It will be medicine, too, with the single largest phase 1 clinical trial ever in human history by mandate. And, you never mandate nor obligate, a human. Only the politics ideology enslaves. Remember better living through chemistry? When you feed it to your body, your body stops doing it, itself, and we're weaker as a result. Or, how about just the "what's wrong with science being popular, or even profitable" schtick? Because when its popular, it's politics. And, when it's profitable, it's a business. And, then, the last thing it is in either event, is science.

We could industrial-strength Band-Aid these symptoms of the problem all day long as we have been doing, with legislation, and rules, and whatever else we've thrown at our digital and data and ethics and morality and science and technology and et al. misery, but that doesn't address the problem, which is always money. The pursuit and acquisition thereof. And legislative Band-Aids, or more ideologue bluster about how to act regarding such matters, most certainly, are not progress, industrial-strength, or otherwise.

The Empirical Evidence

Throughout this work, extraordinary claims are met with extraordinary evidence, both empirical and physical, substantiating these claims. The sweeping arc of human history—from the rise and fall of empires to the cyclical booms and busts of economies, and the endless wars fought over ideological lines—forms a clear and recurring pattern. Yet, the practical explanations and examples making up the system of all human misery are so obvious to human reason as to be irrefutable and undeniable, despite what the Age of the Swindle would try to convince us of otherwise.

WORLD PEACE

Drawing on ecological theory, Robert T. Paine's concept of the "keystone species" is invoked as an analogy: every system depends critically on one key element, whose removal results in systemic change. In the case of the system of all human misery, the keystone is the money tool for the first ideology itself: monetary economy.

Remove belief in these ideological fictions, and the entire oppressive system becomes more amenable for all life, peacefully. Politics, for instance, only exists to make money. And we know that since no politics ever solved anything or we'd be at peace already. Remove money, then, and what's politics to do? Exactly what the majority have already told politics to do: nothing. See Figure 2 for all evidence of that.

Most encouragingly, though, this change requires no violent upheaval, no revolution, and no change to daily life. Instead, it demands only the collective decision to cease participation in the fiction (Estes et al., 2016).

However, empirical evidence and systemic theory reveal that money—the keystone in the system of all human misery—can be removed, resulting in peaceful systemic change, should humanity collectively choose to abandon these fictions at no cost.

This work invites you to join the majority of humans, recognize the Age of the Swindle for what it is and embrace the power of collective awakening and non-participation any longer and world peace.

The Anthropogenic Imperative

We are living in a geological epoch that scientists have identified as the Anthropocene—a distinct era marked by the

WORLD PEACE

overwhelming influence of human activity on Earth's ecosystems and geological processes (Biello, 2009; Aeon, 2021). Unlike previous epochs, the Anthropocene is defined by humanity's capacity to alter climate, biodiversity, land, water, and air at global scales when in the pursuit and acquisition of money. The very fabric of the biosphere is being rewritten through our collective actions. The very wobble of the Earth impacted by our megalithic appetites.

This era coincides with what scientists have termed the sixth mass extinction—a rapid, unprecedented loss of species diversity caused predominantly by human-induced factors resulting in trash. Habitat destruction, pollution, overexploitation, and the spread of invasive species are driving countless plants and animals toward extinction at rates estimated to be hundreds to thousands of times higher than natural background levels. And, all for a paycheck, or the ravages of warfare. This loss of biodiversity not only threatens individual species but imperils the complex ecological relationships and services essential for life on Earth, including human survival.

The "clock is ticking." The window to prevent irreversible damage is narrowing dramatically. Without decisive change, these trends portend a cascade of ecological collapse, threatening food security, clean water availability, disease regulation, and climate stability. In this context, the continuation of the current systemic patterns—rooted in the ideological fiction of money and politics—will exacerbate planetary instability, hastening not only human suffering but the potential extinction of any other organisms to survive us within 800 years after we're gone.

It is our fault, too. All our faults. For 13,000 years, in fact. If we are ever to be the truly virtuous species that God had intended us to be (whomever you hold God to be, by whatever name it is that you call God) then it is incumbent upon us to simply snap out of it, sound off to the POICC, and come on in for the big win to get something done with this place for the last 3% to survive us. We are finished. Nothing will save us. And nothing to survive us will ever remember us. This is the greatness of the human species. We do this to prove ourselves worthy to have existed at all, by planting the seed for what comes next, and then exit this life, arm in arm, having one another's backs, as siblings in the last iteration of human in our family of Man.

Ending the Swindle is not simply a moral or ethical ideal; it is a biological and ecological imperative. The systems that govern production, consumption, governance, and conflict must be radically transformed to align with planetary limits rather than relentless growth and division. The prevailing ideologies of profit maximization, political power struggles, and resource exploitation have pushed natural systems beyond safe thresholds, blind to the interconnectedness of life and the finite nature of Earth's resources.

These products created from the Age of the Swindle that end up as trash bear little relevance on the persistence of the human species, though, beyond perhaps how bad life will suck until we die from those products. In the whole biological fight against extinction, just with these waste products from the Age of the Swindle, humans have an additional straw to bear. Beyond trash and ecology and all the rest of it, or extinction is the result of a genetic threshold we crossed about 150 years ago from which there is no return.

It's irreversible and irrecoverable. But it also makes us all siblings in the family of Man for the last thousand years we

WORLD PEACE

have left. We are, all of us, the same. And, we all have the same capacity for all the virtue, honor, nobility, wisdom, and imagination necessary to accomplish whatever advanced problem-solving is required, once the crushing repression of ideological fiction is eliminated from human consciousness.

World peace, therefore, transcends its common perception as a lofty, optional aspiration or diplomatic goal. It is the only viable pathway toward securing humanity's long-term persistence and ecological redemption. Peace in this vision encompasses more than the absence of war; it includes restoring reason within human societies and rationale between humans and the natural world. This is going to be important if we are to terraform Earth into something habitable again.

This imperative implies collective recognition of our shared fate as a species and as stewards of the planet. It demands shifting from adversarial and extractive systems toward cooperative approaches grounded in respect for empirical reality, ecological balance, sustainability, and shared well-being. Abolish money and that is precisely what results, and nothing changes for Man, except that our receipts read 0.00, and no more trash.

To fail in ending the Age of the Swindle and achieving true peace is to risk writing the final chapter of human history in tragedy—one marked by collapse, extinction, and loss. To succeed is to create a new epoch, not defined by human dominion but by humble stewardship, virtuous coexistence, and flourishing for all life. We already did that successfully for 200,000 years, anyway, prior to "the great burn" as the gifting system of economy – predicated on physical reality – of commonly held value for our birthrights of potable water, biogenic elements, and the ability to raise fire.

The evidence is clear: the choices made now will determine whether humanity is remembered as the cause of the planet's demise or the architect of its redemption. Embracing this anthropogenic imperative is the urgent call of our times. Contribute your submission to the POICC and this world can be at peace in, literally, less than one day. (And, no need to send them all on the same day. Just saying, not good). 35 days from the publication of this work, the clock starts. When the POICC gets its majority voice on the matter, job well done. So, no need to bring down their servers on the first day, or jam their mailboxes so fast that we put half their mailroom staff on oxygen to keep up. This should be fun. And all of us absolved and all those before us redeemed in this single act. So, treat your submission with at least as much reverence as was afforded putting the first footprints on the Moon. You're electing the new age of freedom and 1,000 years of peace.

Conclusion: The First Step

Understanding the Age of the Swindle is not merely an intellectual exercise—it is the crucial inaugural step on the path to ending the systemic misery that has plagued humanity for millennia. This understanding involves a profound recognition: the complex systems that govern our societies—money, politics, corporations, countries—are not inevitable fixtures of human existence, nor are they natural laws inscribed into the fabric of reality. Instead, these are social constructs, ideological fictions, sustained solely through collective belief and participation.

These systems, while seemingly immutable, were created by humans and, therefore, can be unmade or abandoned by human agency. The revelation that these constructs are fictions is liberating, for it reveals that we are not prisoners

WORLD PEACE

bound by destiny or nature, but participants with the power to choose what we accept as real and authoritative. We simply stop participating in our own enslavement.

World peace, contrary to common skepticism, is not a utopian dream lost beyond reach or a mere fantasy for idealists. It is a deeply practical and attainable outcome. Achieving it depends fundamentally on ending the Age of the Swindle—the collective acceptance of these ideological fictions that generate division, conflict, inequality, and suffering as the system of all human misery.

By choosing to see through the illusion—to perceive the difference between empirical reality and imposed fiction—we open the door to a new social order. A next age, predicated on human freedom, and 1,000 years of peace, as the natural humans again with tendencies toward rational right actions and advanced problem-solving and virtues. It's how our species succeeded for 200,000 years, before "the great burn". This choice requires courage and clarity, as it means confronting long-standing beliefs and vested interests that benefit from the current arrangements, and overcoming the inertia of habit and fear.

It is important to remember that the power we bestow the system of all human misery derives entirely from our belief in it (Szasz, 1973; Zmigrod, 2021). Like all fictions, once recognized as such, it loses its mystique and authority. The mental and social hold this illusion has had over individuals and societies weakens and eventually dissolves under the light of critical awareness. This is why the POICC has made submissions to them so easy, and it's not like they aren't already expecting your submissions after 12 years of hearing it from me, already. And, if nothing else but for my part in

WORLD PEACE

this family of Man, as my siblings – whoever you are – I got you. So, no fear or apprehension, just family.

The implications of this awakening are profound: when enough of us collectively withdraw our belief and participation, the Age of the Swindle ceases to function as a system of control. This does not necessitate violent revolution or destructive upheaval. Activism is never advocacy. Instead, it is a peaceful de-ideologization and collective realignment toward reality, which is both natural and restorative (Estes et al., 2016). So, contribute your voice and advocate for your freedom

The Age of the Swindle—a long historical period characterized by ideological fictions masquerading as realities—can come to an end, yielding to a new age: an age grounded in empirical truth, respect for human dignity, cooperation, and genuine freedom, but most notably, absent any system of all human misery. This emergent era would be defined by peace, stability, and human reason, as the conative toxin, mental malady of greed, division, and false knowledge dissipate.

This is not just a hopeful vision but a practical strategy grounded in historical precedent, scientific evidence, and ethical clarity. The first step—understanding—is accessible to all, and it catalyzes the possibility of a future where peace is the natural condition, not the exception.

Chapter 2: Historical Foundations and Ideological Origins

Some Background

The story of humanity's social and economic evolution is one marked by profound transformation, shifting from concrete, communal modes of living to abstract systems governed by collective imagination and ideology. To appreciate the full magnitude of this change, we must first understand the foundational social dynamics of early human societies, where economic and social life were deeply intertwined and motivated by principles far removed from the impersonal market transactions that dominate today.

Early Economic Systems: Gifting and Barter

In the earliest epochs of human existence, economic interactions were related to gifting and barter systems that extended beyond mere transactional exchanges. Figure 1 illustrates the approximate rise for each of these economies. These systems were relational and reasonable frameworks, deeply rooted in trust, and mutual participation, yet no expectation of reciprocity. The act of giving served a social purpose—to reinforce bonds of kinship, trust, and communal solidarity, rather than to secure immediate return or profit. It is a naturally occurring expression for many organisms: sharing. Brokered at the time were most frequently our birthrights as the needful things for all life. Commonly held value that promotes survival as opposed to the commonly agreed-upon value that drives profits. Anthropological studies of indigenous societies continue to reveal how gifting forms a vital social glue, regulating relationships and ensuring group cohesion (Aeon, 2017a; Aljazeera, n.d.-a).

Interactions between larger groups or socially distant individuals or natural disasters or potentially any number of other influences could have led to the development of barter—the direct exchange of goods and services without a standardized intermediary. However, barter still rested fundamentally on notions of mutual benefit and shared humanity, where exchanges reflected immediate needs and personal relationships, rather than abstract market logic (BBC, 2017a).

Minimal Social Stratification and Ownership

Crucially, archaeological and ethnographic evidence indicates that early human groups typically exhibited minimal social stratification. The concepts of private or formalized ownership, hierarchical social classes, and institutionalized violence were not widespread. Instead, the default mode was one of shared resources, collective survival strategies, and egalitarian social relations (CNN, 2018; BBC, 2017b).

Such social arrangements were naturally conducive to peace and cooperation, as claims to property or social status were limited or non-existent. Resources were evaluated primarily on utility and necessity, rather than symbolic or financial worth—a fact that underscores the deeply different value systems at play before ideology's ascendancy.

The Radical Transformation: From Tangible to Abstract

The transition from these tangible, relational systems to those based on commonly agreed-upon abstract value—the monetary economy—was not a seamless or inevitable

WORLD PEACE

evolution but a radical transformation in human consciousness and social stratification. This fundamental shift inaugurated what can be termed the "Age of the Swindle", characterized by the prioritization of abstract concepts and collective fictions over material and communal realities (Aeon, 2017b; Aeon, 2017c).

Money's invention was driven by the practical challenge of facilitating exchange across expanding human networks in which gifting and/or barter became inconvenient or impossible. It was, likely, an extinction-level event that occurred some 13,000 years ago, and human invention simply rose to the occasion to keep the gifting supply chain functioning.

Biogenic elements, potable water, and the ability to raise fire are the only 3 things humans need in order to live anywhere in the universe. Literally. Yet, remove even 1 of those, and humans can't even exist on Earth. After "the great burn", humans lost 2. We had everything in place already, we just couldn't drag our chickens, cows, and dogs across that howling frigid wilderness of ash. But, if I use this seashell to represent a purse full of chickens, and that seashell to represent a pocket full of cows, I can get across that wilderness to the picnic table myself. Then, I just got to get the Broker to understand. And, it saved us.

Early forms of money, such as shells, salt, or elephant tail, served as currency tools to overcome barters and gifting's limitations—portable, divisible, and widely accepted instruments (OpenStax, 2023). However, the profound innovation lay not in the physical trade coins themselves but in their symbolic function.

Money does not possess intrinsic value; rather, it is a universal translation tool for value. This shift effectively introduced a new layer of abstraction—economic value detached from direct physical utility, becoming a social and psychological construct (Numbeo, n.d.).

Ideology as a "Conative Toxin"

The rise of money catalyzed the emergence of ideology—systems of belief and practice that exist not in natural reality but within the shared imagination of societies. According to Aeon (2017d; 2017e), ideology operates as a form of "conative toxin": a fiction made palpably 'real' through rules, tools, and legal structures, then sustained through ongoing collective participation and the willful suspension of disbelief (Aeon, 2017f).

This process of suspending disbelief is not simply passive ignorance but an active cultural practice—a collective agreement to treat these fictions as objective truths, enabling large-scale social coordination but also facilitating alienation and exploitation. Humans are advanced problem-solvers, rational reasonable actors, virtuous to a fault. Only by living fiction, as if it were real, could Man undermine those qualities that ensured our survival. Hence, industrial accident. And it killed us.

Psychological and Social Impacts of the Transition

The adoption of money and ideology was not just an economic innovation but a psychological transformation. Where formerly value was derived from survival, sharing, and mutual aid, it increasingly became about accumulation, competition, and domination (Worldwatch Institute, n.d.; Grens, 2011).

Humans may well be rational reasonable actors, when absent ideological bent. But we are also extremophiles. Figure 3 in the appendix provides examples, but humans do a lot of things that other organisms do, we just take it one step further than any other organism on the planet. Other organisms do trust. We do, too, to the extent of faith. Other organisms do value. For us, it extends to love. Almost all other organisms in the natural world do economy. And, we take it to greed. These new economic imperatives altered interpersonal relations fundamentally. The emphasis on accumulation fostered greed and rivalry, disrupting prior social norms that emphasized unilateral egalitarianism. This shift sowed seeds of unequal power dynamics, social stratification, and systemic injustice, which have intensified over millennia.

The Rise of Bureaucracy and Institutionalization

Parallel to this transformation was the emergence of bureaucracy—formalized systems of administration designed to organize, oversee, and regulate the new abstract government, born of the natural human tendency for governance, (and we're exceptional at it). Bureaucracy introduced layers of rules, hierarchies, and procedures that often obscure original communal intentions of governance and equitable resource distribution (Wikipedia, n.d.-a; OpenStax, 2023; SocialSci LibreTexts, 2023).While bureaucratic systems were intended to enhance order and predictability, their proliferation frequently breeds inefficiency, alienation, and detachment from the governed communities. Through infusion of ideology into bureaucracy over time, citizens become reduced to numbers or data points within an impersonal machine, undercutting the relational foundations that characterized earlier societies.

Modern Consequences: Imbalances and Injustices

The need for universally recognized systems of value and control also necessitated international covenants and agreements, aiming to address emerging imbalances and injustices rooted in these new ideological frameworks. Examples include instruments such as the International Covenant on Economic, Social and Cultural Rights, which seeks to codify protections and rights within the abstract economic-political order (Wikipedia, n.d.-b).

Yet, these frameworks remain constrained within the irrationality of ideology—striving to regulate fictions rather than simply dismantling the foundational systems themselves. Industrial-strength Band-Aids, as it were. As a result, many structural injustices persist or worsen, entrenching disparities and systemic misery.

The easiest, most efficient, and effective means for eliminating a problem, is to eliminate the problem. That has, literally, always worked, everywhere on Earth, for all of time. It can't be much simpler. If money is your problem, for instance, get rid of your problem. Instantly, economy becomes infinitely less complicated, far more sustainable, and unilateral egalitarian distribution unincumbered.

Ideologies Aside

WORLD PEACE

First, humans do ideology; individually. And, that's fine. No one can tell you what to think, any more than they can tell you how to feel. These are our human rights. It's why we value trustworthy knowledge. (It's a right too). It is only when ideology becomes structured, orchestrated, scripted that humans can buffoon along with the organized, and/or institutionalized rules, and/or tools, and/or codes of law. This is the ideology that became our first industrial accident. The conative toxin that began with monetary economy, upon which, all other organized, and/or institutionalized ideologies are reliant. Get rid of money, and all other organized, and/or institutionalized ideology fades away along with it. But humans retain individual ideology, where it should be.

To fully grasp the profound impact of the historical shift from tangible communal economies to abstract ideological systems, it is essential to examine the nature of ideology itself—not merely as a collection of ideas or beliefs but as a powerful and often invisible system that compels human action and shapes societies. Ideology functions as a conative force: it influences desires, motivations, and behaviors, structuring social order and becoming increasingly self-reinforcing and resistant to change over time (Aeon, 2017g; Aeon, 2017h).

At its core, ideology operates by making fiction appear real. Through the creation and enforcement of rules, tools, and laws, however, societies structure those abstract concepts into seemingly reasonable practices—such as property, wealth, authority, and country—and impose them as if they were natural facts. The nation is not the country, for instance. Country is a map, lines on the ground, drawn for an ideology; the nation exists within each of us as an identity. Patriot is not partizan. Partizan is an ideology party an affiliation; patriot is a product of national identity.

These fictions do not exist outside the collective imagination, however, yet they become embedded so deeply that individuals must act as if these constructs are objective realities (Aeon, 2017i). Even truth is not accuracy. Accuracy is the cold, hard, calculable, quantifiable fact of the matter. Truth is everyone's individual stories of those facts. Truth, then, is said to be purely source dependent, (...that's "my truth", as it were). This collective participation—this willful suspension of disbelief—is critical; without it, organized, and/or institutionalized ideology cannot sustain itself. Further, there must be divisiveness, a "them" and "us", or a "haves" and "have nots" for ideology to work. It's why humans prefer to keep ideology to themselves. We mind our manners and we keep or friends, as it were.

The fundamental problem with ideology is not merely its falsity but rather its imposition on the material reality of human existence. When fiction is allowed to dictate social and economic relations, it often results in catastrophic consequences: division, conflict, systemic oppression, and widespread suffering (Aeon, 2017j; The Age of Consequences, 2016).

This emergence of organized, and/or institutionalized ideology can be seen as the first "industrial accident" in human consciousness—a byproduct of our unique human capacities for imagination and abstraction (Aeon, 2017k; Aeon, 2017l). While these capacities have enabled innovation and adaptation, they also risk detaching us from empirical reality.

WORLD PEACE

Social Stratification and Violence Linked to Ideology

Anthropological and historical research aligns the rise of ideology with the advent of social stratification, organized violence, and systemic inequality (BBC, 2017c; CNN, 2017a). As money, greed and other mental maladies assumed central roles in the formation of civilization, new forms of hierarchy and control emerged. Control over monetary systems, political power structures, or religious institutions enabled certain groups to accumulate disproportionate resources and influence, frequently at the expense of wider community welfare (Aljazeera, n.d.-b; NPTrust, n.d.).

A significant implication of ideology was the introduction of scarcity as a civil construct rather than an absolute natural condition. This permitted the social stratification of civilization and eventually the concept of industrial slavery by extension. By assigning symbolic value to objects and resources, societies manufactured artificial divisions between "haves" and "have-nots," fueling competition, exclusion, and conflict where none had necessarily existed before (OpenStax, 2023; Numbeo, n.d.; Worldwatch Institute, n.d.).

Notably, archaeological records indicate an absence of organized warfare prior to the rise of governments and formalized property rights (CNN, 2018; BBC, 2017b). While that statement is accurate about the first war being 8,100 years ago, there is one issue to point out. Archeologists, just like the rest of us, only believe that there is such a thing as property rights. That's just more ideology rules, eventually codified into human consciousness, and propagated relentlessly tantamount to genetic memory, since the Devine Rights of Kings. But that still doesn't make it real. Without an original manufacturer's receipt, we all own this planet. Equally. Equitably.

Only ideology could make humans believe otherwise. No kings, no corporations, no conquerors, no discoverers, just humans, as the only suitable stewards and custodians of the same. Regardless, even if you "own" you house, in the US, at least, you only own it 99 years, then you got to buy it again. The system of all human misery in full bloom, as it were. Well, you can't have war, either, without country. Indeed, the ideology of politics, emerging contemporaneously with that of monetary economy, depended fundamentally on divisiveness for its persistence. This divisiveness not only justified war but institutionalized conflict as a regular feature of human society (The Age of Consequences, 2016; Aljazeera, n.d.-a).

Institutionalization through Bureaucracy

The rise of bureaucratic systems further entrenched these ideologies within the architecture of modern states and organizations. Designed to bring order and efficiency, bureaucracies often evolve into self-serving entities that prioritize their own perpetuation over the genuine needs of the people (Wikipedia, n.d.-a; SocialSci LibreTexts, 2023). This institutionalization reinforces the dominance of abstract systems (money, politics, administration) over the lived reality of individuals (Wikipedia, n.d.-a; OpenStax, 2023). When I say that 'we don't need to fill those seats every election cycle', it is exclusively because we have bureaucracy. We just need to run it absent ideology. And that's worldwide. Countries might have their own unique ideological bents, but bureaucracy is veritably identical in the servicing of ~150 nations. So, we can elect to be free again this election cycle, by not subjugating ourselves to another, and let the bureaucracy keep the lights on and wheels of progress turning as designed.

Mechanisms of Persistence and Psychological Effects

Once established, ideology shows remarkable resilience, a persistence rooted in early and continuous programming of individuals to accept ideological fictions as reality. From childhood, education systems, media, and cultural norms embed these beliefs deeply, making them difficult to question or resist (Aeon, 2017m; BBC, 2017d). In any other context, that would constitute child abuse.

The monetary economy, in particular, precipitated the emergence of greed as a mental malady—a uniquely human pathological desire inspired solely by money. Unlike other desires tied to survival or reproduction, greed is characterized by an endless longing for "more," unmoored from natural limits. It exacerbates existing psychological dysfunctions, as well, such as egomania from power and narcissism from celebrity.

Efforts to challenge ideological systems frequently encounter entrenched resistance, fueled by cognitive biases such as the Backfire Effect, (Craig Silverman, CJR, 17, 2011) where individuals cling to familiar but harmful fictions even when confronted with contradictory evidence (Aeon, 2017o). This psychological inertia perpetuates the dominance of ideology despite its demonstrable contribution to misery and dysfunction. Maybe it shouldn't come as any surprise, then, that the powers that be have known about this for 12 years, and still no substantive change. I suppose their waiting on the majority voice, too.

The Hidden Anatomy of Oppression

The cumulative result is a self-reinforcing system of all human misery—an invisible, pervasive framework that shapes the global social order (Aeon, 2017p). This system systematically represses human virtues such as honor, nobility, wisdom, and imagination—qualities that have historically defined our humanity but are marginalized or nullified by the demands of conformity and obedience to ideological rules (Aeon, 2017q; Aeon, 2017r).

Conformity is prized above creativity; obedience above compassion (Aeon, 2017s; BBC, 2017a). Is a slave actually a slave if they don't know what slavery is? Consequently, billions live under the psychological and material burdens imposed by the ideologies of money and politics. Whether through economic enslavement or political subjugation, the vast majority are denied fundamental freedoms and the dignity that should be their birthright (International Covenant on Economic, Social and Cultural Rights, n.d.; Aljazeera, n.d.-b; NPTrust, n.d.).

Particularly disturbing are those facts since the planet is largely majority rule, and the majority on the planet don't do politics. By 60% consistently. Yet those seats of power get filled, the world over, every election cycle, despite the fact that the majority of humans consistently elect to be free. And you can see Figure 2 for all evidence of that, in the US, at least. So, while other countries might obfuscate their election metrics, statistics works, and the winner-take-all system of American democracy makes election metrics crystal clear. So, statistically, it's 60% the world over.

Ecological and Existential Threats

In the current Anthropocene epoch, with scientific consensus confirming the ongoing sixth mass extinction, the persistence of ideological systems underpins not only human suffering but also threatens planetary survival (World Health Organization, 2014; United Nations Environment Program, n.d.; Planet Ocean, 2012; BBC, 2017e; Bradford, 2017; California Coastal Commission, n.d.; Chambers, 2011; Blacksmith Institute & Green Cross, n.d.; U.S. EPA, n.d.-a, n.d.-b; Grens, 2011; ScienceDaily, 2007; Yale, 2017; Time, 2013; BBC, 2017f; BBC, 2017g; CNN, 2017c; GoodPlanet, n.d.; LiveScience, n.d.).

These ideologies underpin systems of exploitation and environmental destruction, locking humanity into unsustainable patterns that imperil countless species, and flagrantly stand in the way of sustainability.

Possibility and Pathway to Liberation

Despite this grim reality, hope remains. Every complex system hinge on a keystone component—a critical element whose removal triggers transformative change. For the global system of human misery grounded in ideology, that keystone is money (Aeon, 2017t).

By collectively "setting all general ledgers to zero"—abolishing money as a controlling fiction—humanity can peacefully dissolve the ideological structures that have constrained us for millennia. This does not require violence or social upheaval, but rather a collective recognition that these fictions serve no necessary purpose in a world whose members seek justice, prosperity, and achievement.

Freed from the repression of ideology, humans can reclaim their reputation as rational, reasonable, and virtuous actors. The qualities that defined our species for hundreds of thousands of years—cooperation, creativity, compassion—can once again become the foundation of social life (Aeon, 2017u; Aeon, 2017v; BBC, 2017a).

The transition away from ideology begins with awareness—understanding the historical and anthropological roots of our present condition and refusing participation in the fictions that sustain systemic misery. Each individual's awakening and choice contribute to a collective movement toward a world where human suffering is no longer systemic and where world peace is not only possible but inevitable. Then, the transition away from ideology culminates with the contribution of your voice to the POICC

Conclusion

The historical foundations and ideological origins of human society reveal a profound and sobering pattern characterized by unintended consequences that have constrained the true potential of our species. What originally began as systems rooted in survival, mutual aid, and cooperation—expressed through practices like gifting and reciprocal barter exchange—gradually transformed into complex ideological structures that fractured social cohesion and sowed division, exploitation, and widespread misery (Aeon, 2017a; Aljazeera, n.d.-a; BBC, 2017a).

This transformation was motivated by practical necessity—the challenge of perpetuating the distribution of birthrights, globally, while coordinating with large and complex social groups—but it also introduced a radical shift in human consciousness. The invention and institutionalization of money as a shared symbolic construct marked the birth of ideological systems, which became embedded in civilization, laws, and governance as conative toxins— fictions that, through collective acceptance and enforcement, gained the power to shape behavior and social structures profoundly (Aeon, 2017d; Aeon, 2017f).

As ideology took hold, previously relational and equitable communities became stratified by new forms of civil hierarchy and oppression, instituted through the concepts of property, authority, and scarcity—none of which are natural givens but social constructs enforced through systems of power (BBC, 2017c; CNN, 2017a; OpenStax, 2023). This ideological foundation institutionalized social inequality and conflict, giving rise to systemic divisions that have shaped the violent and exploitative dynamics of human societies ever since (The Age of Consequences, 2016; Aljazeera, n.d.-a).

Moreover, as bureaucratic systems emerged, layering technical administration over these ideological foundations, the alienation of individuals from their communities intensified, reinforcing the dominance of abstract systems over lived reality and weakening human virtues such as honor, nobility, wisdom, and imagination—qualities once central to humanity's flourishing (Wikipedia, n.d.-a; SocialSci LibreTexts, 2023; Aeon, 2017q; Aeon, 2017r).

However, the story of human suffering within ideology is not a tale of inevitability or eternal doom. We simply force the nonsense to make sense, even if we recognize it as counterintuitive; the first sign that a swindle is at hand. It is, crucially, a call to awareness with an eye on urgency. Then, just pick up a pen, or drop an email to the POICC, and it is as simple as that to turn it all off. Understanding ideology as a conative toxin—a destructive mental and social force perpetuated by collective belief—opens the way to recognizing the possibility of liberation (Aeon, 2017g; Aeon, 2017h; Aeon, 2017p).

Archaeological and anthropological evidence strongly suggests that prior to these ideological constructs, humanity thrived through cooperative and peaceful arrangements lasting for tens of thousands of years without the scourges of organized warfare or systemic inequality (CNN, 2018; BBC, 2017b). This historical legacy is our birthright—the baseline from which the species can reclaim its true nature and rightful status among all life.

The keystone of this entire system—the critical element whose presence sustains the whole system of human misery—is money (Aeon, 2017t). Money's role as an abstract, collective fiction enables the ideological webs of power, scarcity, and competition that bind humanity to cycles of suffering. By collectively choosing to "set all general ledgers to zero"—literally abolishing money as a source of control—we can initiate a fundamental systemic collapse of these toxic ideologies without violence or upheaval (Estes et al., 2016; Aeon, 2017t).

Freed from the constraints imposed by ideological fictions, humanity can reawaken the virtues of cooperation, creativity, wisdom, and compassion that have sustained humans for hundreds of millennia (Aeon, 2017u; Aeon, 2017v; BBC, 2017a). This shift would restore the agency and dignity deprived by political and economic ideologies, enabling civilization to reorganize organically around tangible realities and shared human values rather than abstract fictions intended to divide us.

In a time of profound ecological and existential crisis—the Anthropocene sixth mass extinction—the urgency of this transformation cannot be overstated (Biello, 2009; Aeon, 2021; World Health Organization, 2014; United Nations Environment Program, n.d.). The continuation of ideologies that drive environmental destruction and social imbalance threatens not only human persistence but that of the entire biosphere.

So, with understanding comes hope. By grasping the nature of ideology as a pathology of collective imagination, and by identifying its keystone as being money and removing it, we possess a clear, practical path to reclaiming humanity's greatness. Just write to the POICC. The future of humanity is not bound by the fictions of division and exploitation, but can be rewritten through awareness, choice, and collective action.

In conclusion, the challenge before us is both monumental and achievable. But not as challenging as you might think, unless you were counting on Band-Aiding more symptoms of our problem, again. Then, world peace would be insurmountable. We can chart a new course by shedding the illusions that have enslaved us and by embracing the empirical reality of shared existence. In doing so, world peace—long treated as an elusive dream—can become a practical, living reality. This new era will be defined not by the control of abstract ideology but by the liberation of

WORLD PEACE

human potential, grounded in truth, compassion, and cooperation.

Chapter 3: The Spread of Fictional Systems

Introduction

Ideologies—complex systems of beliefs and values—have been central to human societies throughout history. These systems, though often perceived as objective truths, are essentially fictional constructs created to organize social life, justify power structures, and influence human behavior. Understanding how these fictional systems spread, become entrenched in institutions, and shape individual and collective behavior is crucial for navigating the modern world. This chapter explores the evolution and transmission of ideologies, the mechanisms by which people are "programmed" to accept them, and the challenging process of "deprogramming" necessary to reclaim rationality and virtue.

Building on this foundation, it is important to recognize that ideologies operate through a combination of psychological, cultural, and social processes that embed them deeply into the human experience. From early childhood, individuals are exposed to narratives and symbols that frame their worldview, often transmitted through family, education, media, and religion. This early exposure creates cognitive frameworks that filter information and shape perceptions, making ideologies appear natural and self-evident. Social reinforcement through community and institutional validation further solidifies these beliefs, as dissenting views are marginalized or suppressed. Isn't Jonny's Junior Achievement award industrious, and isn't little Janie's lemonade stand cute, and even a five-year-old knows the Marshmellow test.

WORLD PEACE

The entrenchment of ideologies in institutions—government, legal systems, educational curricula, and economic structures—ensures their persistence and reproduction across generations. These institutions not only perpetuate the ideology but also allocate resources and privileges in ways that maintain the status quo, often benefiting those in power. Consequently, ideologies become tools for social control, legitimizing hierarchies and norms that might otherwise be contested. Ideology created the Doomsday Clock, for instance. But it's been the majority citizens, the world over, who don't do politics, that have kept it from striking twelve.

Deprogramming from deeply ingrained ideologies is a complex and often fraught process. It requires critical self-reflection, exposure to alternative perspectives, and a willingness to question foundational beliefs. The journey toward reclaiming rationality and virtue involves disentangling genuine ethical principles from ideological distortions, enabling individuals and societies to act more authentically and justly. In a rapidly changing world, developing the capacity to critically analyze and adapt one's beliefs is not only desirable but necessary for fostering open, pluralistic, and resilient communities.

Ultimately, the study of ideologies reveals that although they are human-made constructs without inherent facts or evidence, their power lies in their pervasive influence on thought and behavior. By understanding their origins, mechanisms, and effects, individuals can better navigate the challenges of modern life, advocate for freedom, and contribute to the creation of more conscious and adaptable social systems. Seems quite the daunting task for deprogramming, I'm sure. But in the case of our system, we simply pull the keystone, snap out of it collectively, and do nothing any differently than we do today to have everything we'll need tomorrow. The system simply becomes more amenable to all life.

I. Some Foreknowledge: Foundations of Fictional Systems

The Cognitive and Social Origins of Ideology

Human beings are uniquely predisposed to create and internalize complex belief systems. Our personal ideologies. These ideological frameworks begin to form even before birth. Research shows that fetuses in the womb start processing auditory stimuli, including the rhythms and intonations of language, which primes them for later socialization (Aeon, 2017). This early cognitive attunement lays the groundwork for the absorption of cultural narratives and social norms—foundational components of ideology— that guide perception, thought, and behavior throughout life.

From birth onward, humans enter intricate social environments that continually shape and reinforce their ideological understandings. Parents, caregivers, and communities transmit not only explicit knowledge but also implicit values, myths, and symbolic meanings that become deeply entrenched mental frameworks. Through repeated exposure to language, ritual, and storytelling, individuals internalize shared worldviews which serve to organize individual identity and social roles.

Ideologies act as interpretive lenses, simplifying the complex realities of human experience by providing structured narratives about order, morality, power, and meaning, (in the politics ideology, for instance, these are referred to as "bumper sticker slogans"). They offer

WORLD PEACE

cognitive shortcuts that enable individuals to navigate social realities efficiently, yet simultaneously constrain thinking by delineating "acceptable" truths and suppressing alternative perspectives, (again, from the politics ideology, "wedge issues"; no win scenarios intended to obscure options).

Theoretical biology and philosophy have conceptualized this shared mental landscape as the noösphere—a collective sphere of human thought that enshrouds the biosphere with symbolic and conceptual patterns (Compiler Press, n.d.). The noösphere encapsulates how ideas propagate socially and evolve culturally, functioning as an emergent layer where knowledge, beliefs, and ideologies interact, compete, and coalesce to form the fabric of social reality.

Within this noösphere, the mechanisms by which ideologies spread and endure are both cognitive and social in nature. Cognitively, humans possess innate faculties such as pattern recognition, narrative construction, and emotional resonance that facilitate the internalization of ideologies. Socially, institutions—including families, educational systems, religious organizations, and media—act as conduits and gatekeepers that transmit and reify ideological content.

Furthermore, the interconnectedness of individuals within social networks accelerates the diffusion of ideological constructs, reinforcing conformity through social rewards and sanctions. Group identity and the need for belonging amplify this effect, as acceptance often depends on conformity to prevailing ideological norms.

Ideologies also leverage human cognitive biases—such as confirmation bias, in-group favoritism, and authority bias—to entrench themselves further, making them resistant to critical scrutiny or disconfirmation. Over time, these systems become self-perpetuating, evolving through cultural feedback loops where each generation inherits and modifies existing ideological narratives.

Understanding these cognitive and social foundations is critical for grasping how ideologies gain their compelling power, why they are so resilient, and how they ultimately influence both individual psychology and collective behavior at societal scales. Recognizing the noösphere as a living, dynamic realm invites deeper inquiry into the ways human thought shapes and is shaped by the ideological systems that govern societies.

Evolutionary Dynamics of Ideologies

Ideologies are not static; they evolve dynamically in response to changing social, economic, and technological conditions. Granted, they do not evolve nearly as fast, but this evolution resembles biological processes of speciation and extinction, where new ideas emerge, compete, and sometimes replace older ones. Just as species adapt and transform to survive in new environments, ideologies mutate and adapt to persist amid shifting landscapes.

For instance, the transition from agrarian to industrial to knowledge economies has profoundly transformed the dominant ideological narratives about work, value, and human purpose (Peter Bils, 2024). In agrarian societies, ideologies often centered around land stewardship, tradition, and communal survival. With the rise of industrialization, new ideological frameworks emphasized mechanization, production efficiency, and hierarchical labor divisions. More recently, in knowledge and digital economies, ideologies have increasingly valorized innovation, intellectual property, and networked individualism. These shifts

WORLD PEACE

demonstrate how economic phases both induce and are supported by evolving ideological constructs that reorganize fundamental perceptions of identity and societal roles, and evolve into the system of all human misery.

The competitive nature of ideological evolution also results in the survival of the fittest narratives—those most capable of resonating with prevailing power structures, technological possibilities, and cultural anxieties. Some ideologies become dominant not solely based on truth or morality but because they offer practical benefits, psychological comfort, or mechanisms of social control that align with institutional interests.

Institutions such as schools, religious organizations, and media outlets play pivotal roles in transmitting and reinforcing these evolving ideologies. Through rituals, education, and storytelling, institutions embed fictional systems into the collective consciousness, making them appear natural and inevitable (Britannica, 2025). Schools, for example, often systematize dominant ideological perspectives through curricula that emphasize particular historical narratives, values, and social hierarchies, shaping generations' viewpoints and civic identities.

Religious organizations traditionally provide moral frameworks and communal belonging, not only preserving ancient ideologies but also adapting them to contemporary contexts, thereby ensuring continuity and relevance. Media outlets act as powerful accelerants in the diffusion and reinforcement of ideologies by framing events, defining acceptable discourse, and highlighting particular values over others. The convergence of digital media with traditional institutions further accelerates the pace and breadth of

WORLD PEACE

ideological evolution, creating new hybrid narratives and enabling more rapid cultural shifts.

Moreover, technological advancements fundamentally alter the mechanisms of ideological spread and contestation. The internet and social media platforms facilitate the exposure to a diverse array of competing ideologies, but they also create echo chambers and filter bubbles which reinforce the very practice of ideology, let alone ideological polarization. This dynamic encourages the emergence of both syncretic ideologies—blending elements from different traditions—and radicalized forms that reject consensus, making ideological landscapes more fragmented and volatile, yet, seemingly, relevant.

The evolutionary analogy extends to the processes by which ideologies can become extinct or marginalized. Just as species fail when unable to adapt to environmental change, ideologies that do not resonate with new socioeconomic realities or institutional power configurations progressively lose influence. Yet, some vestiges can persist symbolically or culturally without practical relevance, akin to evolutionary relics.

Understanding this evolutionary dynamic is essential for those aiming to critically engage with the ideologies that shape personal and collective realities. This is at the individual level, as well as any organized, and/or institutionalized ideology. It highlights that ideologies are living phenomena, continuously constructed and reconstructed through complex interactions between human conation, institutional reinforcement, and broader societal changes. This awareness opens pathways to more consciously navigate, challenge, or transform ideological systems, rather than passively inheriting them.

WORLD PEACE

The Power of Narrative and Myth

Narratives are the primary vehicles for ideological transmission. From ancient myths to modern media, stories encode values, social roles, and ethical frameworks. These narratives are not merely entertainment; they shape identity, influence behavior, and legitimize social hierarchies (Aeon, n.d.). They function as foundational myths that embed a collective sense of belonging and purpose, anchoring individuals within larger social and political orders.

These stories serve multiple critical functions in society. First, they simplify complex realities into accessible and emotionally resonant forms, making ideologies comprehensible and compelling to diverse audiences. Through narrative structure—conflicts, heroes, villains, and moral lessons—ideologies become embodied in concrete examples rather than abstract principles. This embodiment facilitates emotional investment and moral commitment among adherents.

For example, national myths often construct collective identities that are coopted to justify political boundaries and power relations. Myths of origin, shared struggles, and promises of a common destiny foster cohesion and loyalty, providing moral sanction for the existing political order and its territorial claims. These narratives reinforce citizenship as being privilege and a responsibility, while often defining outsiders or "the other" as threats or lesser beings.

The framing of narratives also determines which voices are heard and which are marginalized. Dominant ideologies often suppress alternative perspectives, maintaining their hegemony through control of cultural production (Wikipedia, n.d.). This control operates through gatekeeping

WORLD PEACE

of literature, education, art, and media, where hegemonic narratives are normalized and dissenting stories sidelined, censored, or discredited.

Moreover, narratives embed cultural assumptions that frame social reality in ways that naturalize inequality and power asymmetries. For instance, meritocratic myths valorize individual effort while obscuring structural barriers that limit opportunity, thus legitimizing social stratification as fair or inevitable. Similarly, myths about racial or ethnic superiority underpin discriminatory ideologies that divide populations and justify exclusion or violence. Such limitations negate the human potential for generalization, and we are all specialists, today, incapable of keeping our own lights on or wheels of progress turning without the right specialist to do so, as a result.

The power of narrative extends beyond overt ideological messaging. Symbolism, metaphor, and archetypal imagery evoke subconscious associations that deepen ideological influence below the level of conscious critique. Educational curricula imbue these narratives early, shaping worldviews before critical faculties mature. Media repetition amplifies narrative saturation, making alternative accounts seem alien or suspect.

The advent of digital media has transformed the dynamics of narrative transmission. On one hand, it democratizes storytelling, enabling marginalized groups to circulate counter-narratives and challenge dominant ideologies. On the other hand, algorithm-driven echo chambers reinforce existing beliefs, polarizing societies and fragmenting the shared symbolic world required for constructive dialogue and social cohesion.

Understanding the power of narrative and myth is crucial for unpacking how ideologies sustain themselves over time and resist change. It reveals that ideological critique must go beyond factual rebuttal to address the deeper emotional and symbolic attachments that narratives create. Only by reconstructing stories that honor human dignity, complexity, and shared interest can societies begin to transcend the divisiveness of organized, and/or institutionalized ideologies and foster genuine inclusion.

II. Programming: How Fictional Systems Shape Human Behavior

Socialization and Conditioning

Programming refers to the systematic processes through which individuals are conditioned to accept and perpetuate ideological systems. Socialization, beginning in early childhood, is the foundational mechanism. Families, schools, and peer groups inculcate dominant values and norms, rewarding conformity and punishing dissent (Aeon, n.d.). This conditioning creates deeply ingrained cognitive and emotional patterns that align individuals with the prevailing ideology, often without conscious awareness.

From the earliest stages of development, children absorb not only language but also the implicit lessons about authority, hierarchy, and social roles embedded within cultural rituals and family interactions. Positive reinforcement for adherence to social norms and ideological expectations fosters a psychological need to conform, while deviation often incurs social sanctions ranging from disapproval to exclusion. Over time, this dynamic embeds ideological beliefs as part of individual identity and worldview, making them resistant to change.

WORLD PEACE

Educational systems act as critical sites for ideological programming. Curricula are frequently designed or influenced to present sanitized or selective historical narratives that reinforce the dominant ideology while excluding or marginalizing dissenting voices, alternative histories, or inconvenient facts (Wikipedia, n.d.). Through textbooks, standardized testing, and instruction, students receive a carefully curated version of reality aligned with prevailing power structures. This shapes collective memory, instills national or cultural identities, and frames political and social norms as natural or inevitable.

Beyond content, pedagogical methods often emphasize rote learning, obedience to authority, and competition rather than critical inquiry or collaborative problem-solving. Such approaches discourage questioning and independent thought, effectively limiting intellectual resistance to ideological assumptions. The formal certification and credentialing processes further legitimize the ideology embedded within education, compelling individual compliance as a condition for social and economic advancement.

Mass media and cultural industries extend programming into adulthood by perpetuating dominant narratives through news, entertainment, advertising, and social media platforms. They often normalize ideological perspectives through repetition and emotional appeal, activating cognitive biases such as confirmation bias and in-group favoritism. Media framing selectively highlights certain issues and omits others, shaping public discourse and reinforcing accepted social hierarchies. These channels also marginalize and censor opposing viewpoints, constraining the spectrum of permissible thought and expression.

Psychologically, repeated exposure to ideological content creates cognitive schemas — mental structures that shape how individuals perceive, interpret, and respond to information and experiences. These schemas streamline cognitive processing but also create blind spots where contradictory evidence is dismissed or distorted. Emotional investment in ideological narratives, often tied to identity and belonging, intensifies resistance to alternative viewpoints, sometimes producing defensive reactions described by social psychologists as the Backfire Effect.

Moreover, programming is often invisible to those subjected to it; because ideologies appear "natural" and self-evident, individuals tend to perceive their beliefs as objective truths rather than socially constructed fictions. This invisibility deepens their hold as individuals rarely question foundational assumptions, lest they risk social alienation or psychological discomfort, provided that foundational assumptions being within the purview of interrogative query even occurred to them.

In sum, socialization and conditioning orchestrated through family, education, media, and culture function as powerful programs that embed fictional systems into human cognition and behavior. These processes sustain ideological dominance by producing populations that unconsciously maintain and reproduce, without question the very systems that shape their realities.

Institutional Reinforcement and Media Influence

Institutions serve as powerful amplifiers and enforcers of ideological programming, embedding specific belief systems deeply within the fabric of society. Legal systems, governments, and corporations do not merely reflect neutral

WORLD PEACE

frameworks; they codify and institutionalize ideological assumptions into policies, laws, and economic structures that shape everyday realities. For example, neoliberal economic ideology strongly influences tax policies and welfare systems, emphasizing market mechanisms, privatization, deregulation, and competition over collective social welfare and redistribution (Amadeo, 2022). This ideological bias often prioritizes corporate interests and financial capital accumulation, perpetuating systemic inequalities and limiting alternative socio-economic models.

Governments legislate and regulate in ways that reinforce the dominant ideology, routinely framing policy debates within the accepted parameters established by prevailing narratives. This can limit public discourse and marginalize dissenting viewpoints or approaches that challenge entrenched power structures. Public institutions themselves often become institutional actors that reproduce ideological tenets through bureaucratic procedures and political practices, creating inertia against transformative change.

Media organizations further entrench these ideologies by framing news, entertainment, and cultural content to align with dominant narratives and power interests. The concept of "manufactured consent," originally articulated by Noam Chomsky and Edward Herman, describes how mass media can subtly shape and manipulate public opinion to support existing social, political, and economic power structures, often without overt coercion (Aeon, n.d.). Through selective story choices, emphasis, language, and omission, media outlets propagate ideological frameworks that become accepted as objective truths or common sense.

The rise of social media platforms, while democratizing access to information, has paradoxically intensified

WORLD PEACE

ideological programming by enabling algorithm-driven content curation. These algorithms prioritize user engagement, often favoring emotionally charged or confirmatory content, which creates echo chambers—closed informational environments that reinforce existing beliefs while filtering out dissenting voices or contrary evidence (Davidow, 2021). This dynamic not only deepens polarization but also reduces critical reflection and encourages tribalistic identities grounded in ideological allegiance.

Furthermore, the integration of media conglomerates with corporate and political interests consolidates ideological influence, as content generation is increasingly governed by profit motives and strategic messaging. The blurring of lines between news reporting, entertainment, advertising, and propaganda complicates efforts to discern truth from constructed narratives, fostering cynicism or uncritical acceptance among audiences.

Institutional reinforcement through media is not monolithic; it often involves complex negotiations and contestations of ideology. Counter-narratives and alternative media exist but typically struggle against the overwhelming structural advantages of dominant institutions. Moreover, the emotional and psychological appeal of dominant ideological narratives, bolstered by repeated media exposure, creates cognitive biases in individuals, such as confirmation bias and motivated reasoning, which entrench ideological commitments even further.

The cumulative impact of institutional reinforcement and media influence is the creation of a self-sustaining feedback loop where ideology is continually reproduced, normalized, and rarely questioned. This cycle obscures the fictional and constructed nature of ideologies, making them appear as immutable social facts, and constrains the collective imagination necessary for envisioning alternative societal paradigms.

Understanding the mechanisms through which institutions and media reinforce ideological systems is essential for developing strategies to disrupt these feedback loops. Greater media literacy, institutional transparency, diversification of informational sources, and fostering critical thinking are crucial steps toward weakening the grip of ideological programming and enabling more open, inclusive, and rational public discourse.

Cognitive and Emotional Mechanisms

At the neurocognitive level, ideological programming profoundly shapes human perception, cognition, and behavior through mechanisms of repeated exposure and emotional reinforcement. The brain's remarkable plasticity enables it to reorganize neural pathways in response to persistent ideological inputs, effectively creating feedback loops that strengthen conformity to dominant belief systems (Zmigrod, 2021). Over time, these neural adaptations solidify ideological commitments, making alternative perspectives cognitively taxing or emotionally unsettling to consider.

Emotional triggers embedded within ideological narratives—such as fear, pride, shame, and hope—serve as potent motivators that anchor individuals to their belief systems, often overriding rational and analytical faculties. For example, fear appeals can heighten perceived threats from "outsiders" or dissenters, fostering in-group cohesion and defensive attitudes, whereas pride in group identity can

WORLD PEACE

cultivate loyalty and self-sacrifice for ideological causes (Al-Ghamdi, 2021). Shame functions as a social regulator, discouraging deviation by associating dissent with personal or group disgrace, thus reinforcing behavioral conformity. These emotional hooks engage the limbic system and subcortical structures, which operate beneath conscious awareness, explaining why ideological adherence can persist even in the face of contradictory evidence.

The advent of the digital age has exponentially amplified the efficiency, scale, and subtlety of ideological programming. Social media platforms employ sophisticated algorithms that curate and personalize content, reinforcing existing beliefs by preferentially exposing users to echo chambers aligned with their preferences and biases (Davidow, 2021). This algorithmic tailoring not only intensifies confirmation bias but also narrows the diversity of information, inhibiting critical reflection and cross-ideological dialogue.

Targeted advertising utilizes behavioral data and psychographic profiling to predict and influence consumer preferences, extending ideological programming from political and cultural domains into everyday economic behaviors. Surveillance technologies, including data mining and biometric analysis, enable unprecedented granularity in monitoring and shaping individual and group behaviors, often without explicit consent or awareness. This manipulation can subtly steer attitudes and decision-making processes—ranging from voting patterns to purchasing habits—at scale and with high precision.

Economically, the cost of influencing human behavior has plummeted, allowing powerful actors to deploy ideological programming campaigns that reach millions of people with minimal expenditure relative to traditional media. This democratization of influence has paradoxical outcomes: while it democratizes voice for some, it can also facilitate the rapid spread of misinformation, propaganda, and divisive narratives engineered to manipulate public sentiment and maintain control.

Moreover, the immersive and continuous nature of digital environments fosters habitual engagement with ideological content, reinforcing neural pathways associated with reward and social validation. Dopaminergic systems are activated through likes, shares, and online recognition, embedding ideological participation as a source of psychological reward and social capital. This biological feedback loop makes disengagement challenging and sustains ideological loyalty even when confronted with disconfirming facts.

In sum, cognitive and emotional mechanisms underlying ideological programming are deeply intertwined with neuroplasticity, affective processing, and technologically mediated amplification. Understanding these mechanisms is essential to developing strategies for critical awareness, resilience, and ultimately, the deprogramming necessary to reclaim independent reason and human virtue in the face of pervasive fictional systems.

Ideological Infection and Polarization

Ideologies spread contagiously through social networks, facilitated by various cognitive biases that shape how individuals receive and process information. Confirmation bias—the tendency to favor information that confirms preexisting beliefs—and groupthink—the drive for conformity within cohesive groups—make individuals more receptive to ideas that align with their existing viewpoints and more dismissive or hostile toward contradictory evidence (ORNL, n.d.). These cognitive tendencies serve as vectors of ideological infection, allowing belief systems to propagate rapidly through social connections and institutional channels.

This infectious spread is amplified by the structure and dynamics of human social networks. People tend to associate with others who share similar values and perspectives, creating homophilic clusters or "echo chambers" where ideological reinforcement occurs continuously without meaningful challenges. As contagion progresses, these reinforcing loops deepen ideological commitment and reduce exposure to alternative viewpoints, accelerating ideological polarization.

Polarization manifests not only as a sociopolitical division but also as a cognitive phenomenon. Individuals' mental frameworks become increasingly ossified, exhibiting rigidity and resistance to reevaluation or modification even when confronted with disconfirming information. This cognitive entrenchment results from neural reinforcement mechanisms whereby repeated activation of belief networks strengthens synaptic connections, making divergent perspectives feel alien or threatening (Al-Ghamdi, 2021).

Such rigidity undermines the foundations of democratic deliberation, which relies on openness, critical dialogue, and willingness to revise opinions. Instead, polarization fosters antagonism, mistrust, and the framing of political or social opponents as existential threats rather than fellow citizens with legitimate concerns. This environment makes compromise difficult and conflict more likely, escalating social tensions and weakening collective problem-solving capacities.

WORLD PEACE

Moreover, polarization complicates the process of deprogramming ideological conditioning. Since entrenched beliefs are intertwined with group identity and emotional attachment, attempts to challenge or question dominant ideologies are often perceived as personal attacks or betrayals, triggering defensive reactions such as cognitive dissonance or motivated reasoning. This not only reinforces ideological echo chambers but can also lead to radicalization or social fragmentation.

The digital age further accelerates these dynamics. Social media algorithms prioritize content that engages emotionally and confirms existing biases, intensifying polarization by exposing individuals predominantly to ideologically congenial materials and filtering out dissent (ORNL, n.d.). The resulting hyper-partisan online environments contribute to real-world divisions, undermining social cohesion and complicating efforts to foster dialogue or consensus.

Understanding ideological infection and polarization as intertwined cognitive and social processes is crucial for developing effective strategies to mitigate their effects. Such strategies might include promoting media literacy to recognize bias, designing social platforms that encourage exposure to diverse viewpoints, fostering intergroup dialogue that builds empathy and reduces perceived threats, and creating institutional frameworks that reward cooperation over conflict.

Ultimately, overcoming ideological polarization requires not only structural reforms but also individual and collective willingness to engage in the arduous journey of deprogramming—reclaiming openness, critical reasoning, and the virtues essential for inclusive and peaceful societies. Or, we could just abolish money and every one of those aforementioned, seemingly insurmountable challenges of institutionalized ideology cease to exist, as what humans do with unincumbered ideology, then, becomes source dependent once again.

Toward Rationality and Virtue

The goal of deprogramming is not simply to reject one ideology for another but to cultivate rationality and virtue as foundational pillars for a more enlightened and humane society. Rationality, in this context, is understood not as a detached or mechanistic form of cold calculation, but as an ongoing, dynamic commitment to truth-seeking, logical coherence, and ethical action in interaction with the world and others (Oxford Academic, n.d.). It requires the capacity to critically evaluate information, identify biases— including one's own—and integrate knowledge in a way that supports wise and just decision-making.

This conception of rationality embraces humility: an awareness of the limitations of one's knowledge, openness to revising beliefs in light of new evidence, and the willingness to engage constructively with alternative perspectives. Such a rational approach counters ideological rigidity by fostering a continuously reflective and adaptive mindset capable of navigating complexity and uncertainty.

Virtue complements rationality by emphasizing the moral character necessary to translate reasoned insight into meaningful action. Cultivating virtues such as empathy, integrity, and courage enables individuals and communities to act in accordance with reasoned principles while respecting the dignity and well-being of others (Aeon, n.d.). Empathy expands one's moral horizon beyond self-interest, promoting understanding and compassion even toward those with divergent views or backgrounds. Integrity ensures consistency between values, beliefs, and behavior, guarding against hypocrisy and enabling trustworthiness. Courage

WORLD PEACE

empowers individuals to uphold truth and justice despite social pressures, fear, or uncertainty.

Educational systems play a crucial role in fostering this integration of rationality and virtue. Beyond rote learning or ideological indoctrination, education must prioritize critical thinking skills that enable learners to analyze arguments, recognize fallacies, and question assumptions. Equally important is the cultivation of emotional intelligence—the ability to perceive, understand, and regulate emotions in oneself and others—which underpins effective empathy and interpersonal communication. Ethical reflection encourages learners to engage with moral dilemmas thoughtfully, developing practical wisdom (phronesis) that guides virtuous conduct in concrete situations.

Such education requires environments that encourage open dialogue, curiosity, and respect for diversity, rather than dogmatic adherence to prescribed doctrines. Creating spaces for collaborative problem-solving and moral discourse prepares individuals to participate actively and responsibly in pluralistic societies. Furthermore, lifelong learning and reflective practice should be emphasized, as rationality and virtue evolve continuously throughout life.

The integration of rationality and virtue is indispensable for the successful deprogramming of ideological conditioning. It enables individuals not only to dismantle limiting beliefs but also to reconstruct frameworks for meaning, identity, and social engagement grounded in reality, ethical reasoning, and shared human values. This foundation supports societal transformation toward more just, peaceful, and sustainable modes of coexistence.

In sum, the journey toward rationality and virtue represents the heart of deprogramming—not a mere intellectual exercise, but a holistic development of mind and character that empowers humans to reclaim autonomy, dignity, and the capacity for honest and compassionate collective life.

Conclusion

Fictional systems—ideologies—are an inescapable and pervasive aspect of human societies, fundamentally shaping perceptions, behaviors, institutions, and collective realities. These complex systems of beliefs and values evolve dynamically, continually responding to and interacting with changing social, economic, and technological conditions. They spread and become deeply embedded through processes of socialization, institutional reinforcement, and cognitive-emotional programming that operate from early childhood throughout one's lifetime (Aeon, n.d.; Britannica, 2025).

While ideologies can provide order, coherence, and a shared sense of meaning, enabling societies to function and individuals to navigate complexity, they also carry profound risks. When left unquestioned or rigidly upheld, fictional systems distort human rationality and erode essential virtues such as wisdom, empathy, and courage (Oxford Academic, n.d.; Aeon, n.d.). The power of narratives and myths to emotionally bind individuals to ideological constructs creates cognitive and social feedback loops that resist critical scrutiny and perpetuate social inequalities, conflict, and systemic injustices (Aeon, n.d.; Wikipedia, n.d.).

Understanding the mechanisms by which ideologies spread—including the roles of education, media, institutions, and digital technologies—is crucial for fostering individual autonomy and collective critical awareness. Cognitive biases such as confirmation bias and the emotional hooks of fear, pride, and shame contribute to ideological "infection," polarization, and rigid mental frameworks that threaten democratic deliberation and social cohesion (ORNL, n.d.; Al-Ghamdi, 2021; Davidow, 2021).

Burl Minnis

WORLD PEACE

Deprogramming—though challenging and fraught with emotional and social risks—is a vital process for reclaiming rationality and ethical agency. It involves consciously questioning and unpacking inherited beliefs, recognizing the fictional and constructed nature of dominant ideologies, and cultivating critical thinking, self-expression, and reflective dialogue (Wikipedia, n.d.; Peterson v. Sorlien, 1980). Deprogramming must also nurture suppressed human virtues such as empathy, integrity, and courage, which empower individuals to act in alignment with reasoned principles beyond mere ideological allegiance (Oxford Academic, n.d.; Aeon, n.d.).

Educational systems that prioritize critical thinking, emotional intelligence, and ethical reflection are foundational to this transformative process. Likewise, fostering supportive communities and alternative frameworks for meaning-making helps individuals navigate the disorientation and vulnerability that often accompany ideological disillusionment (Pulitzer Center, n.d.). The conscious cultivation of rationality and virtue enables not only personal liberation from ideological control but also collective reimagining of social structures based on truth, justice, and shared humanity.

Importantly, recognizing that all ideological systems are mutable constructs opens the possibility for systemic transformation. Removing foundational "keystone" elements—such as the deeply entrenched monetary economy ideology—can trigger cascading changes that dissolve dependent political and social ideologies, paving the way for societies grounded in cooperation, equity, and sustainable well-being (Peter Bils, 2024; Compiler Press, n.d.).

WORLD PEACE

In this light, the task before humanity is both profound and hopeful: to awaken from the grip of fictional systems that have shaped and often constrained human flourishing, and to collaboratively reconstruct social realities that honor rational inquiry, empathy, and virtue as guiding principles. This journey demands courage, patience, and solidarity, but it also promises the realization of more just, peaceful, and resilient futures.

Ultimately, the cultivation of critical awareness and ethical agency is not only an individual imperative but a collective responsibility. By embracing this path, humans can transcend the limitations imposed by ideological fictions and participate actively in co-creating worlds where reason, dignity, and compassion prevail.

Part II
Crimes against Humanity

Chapter 4: A Brief History of Value and the Economy

Introduction

The development of human societies has always been shaped by the concepts of value and economy since the first human civilization some 8,500 years ago, or so. These concepts, deceptively simple on the surface, have evolved into complex systems that profoundly influence human interactions, social structures, and the distribution of resources. We have come far from the natural world definitions and practices of value and economy. While often portrayed as objective measures or neutral frameworks, value and economy are, in fact, deeply entwined with ideology, today, becoming fictional constructs themselves that encode beliefs about worth, exchange, and obligation.

These constructs have not only enabled cooperation and social organization but have also been institutionalized to justify and perpetuate systems of domination and control. Throughout history, the conceptualization of value has shifted dramatically—from communal understandings tied to birthrights, kinship, and shared welfare to abstract representations such as money and markets.

This transformation was not inevitable but emerged through a series of social, cultural, and technological innovations embedded in contextually-specific ideological narratives. As these narratives became institutionalized, they laid the groundwork for modern economies that prioritize profit maximization, competition, and accumulation of capital,

WORLD PEACE

often at the expense of human dignity and ecological sustainability.

The economic systems that arose from these ideological shifts have been implicated in some of the darkest chapters of human history—exploitation of enslaved peoples, colonial plunder, systemic poverty, environmental degradation, and vast inequalities of wealth and power. These consequences reveal how economic ideologies function not merely as organizational tools but as mechanisms of control that mask structural violence behind narratives of merit, efficiency, and progress. Clearly, such crimes against humanity demand the immediate and total cessation of practice.

By tracing the evolution of value and economy across historical epochs—from tribal gift economies and barter systems to monetary markets and capitalist enterprises—this chapter seeks to uncover the ideological roots of contemporary economic injustices. Figure 1 illustrates the timeline of events. Drawing from anthropology, history, and political economy, it foregrounds the ways in which fictional economic constructs have been naturalized as unchallengeable truths, obscuring alternative modes of social cooperation and resource sharing.

Moreover, understanding this historical trajectory is crucial for recognizing that current economic crises—ranging from persistent global poverty to climate change—are not accidents or natural outcomes but products of ideological choices and institutional arrangements. Such insight opens the possibility that alternative economic paradigms, grounded in communal responsibility, equity, and sustainability, might be envisioned and realized as soon as money is no longer the motive.

WORLD PEACE

Ultimately, this chapter aims to provide readers with the conceptual tools to critically engage with the economic ideologies shaping the contemporary world and to inspire deeper inquiry into pathways that can undo the systemic harms perpetuated by entrenched fictional systems of value.

I. A Brief History of Value

The Origins of Value: Communal and Birthright Systems

For most of human history, value was not measured in coins, property titles, or digital ledgers, but in the quality and strength of relationships, the availability of resources for survival, and the overall health and cohesion of the community. Archaeological and anthropological scholarship reveals that early human societies—ranging from nomadic hunter-gatherer bands to settled Neolithic farming communities—operated under markedly different economic and social logics than those prevalent today. These systems were predominantly characterized by social and economic equality, cooperation, and mutual aid, concepts that modern economic frameworks often obscure or devalue (Khan Academy, n.d.; Aeon, 2018a).

In these societies, the allocation of resources was guided primarily by shared needs, kinship ties, and reciprocal relationships rather than individual ownership or competitive acquisition. This was the commonly held value economy, predicated chiefly on birthrights and other needful things for all life to persist, not as a means to accumulate wealth, or with the expectation of reciprocity, but to strengthen social bonds and ensure group survival. Gift-giving was a central practice, symbolizing trust and obligation within the community, and ensuring that

Burl Minnis

WORLD PEACE

resources circulated to where they were most needed (Aeon, 2018a).

Notably, recent anthropological research into Neolithic societies challenges earlier ethnocentric assumptions about social exclusivity. Studies suggest that immigrants or outsiders were frequently integrated and treated as equals within these communities, indicating a social structure deliberately emphasizing inclusion, collaboration, and collective resilience over hierarchical exclusion or ethnic stratification (MSN, 2021). This inclusive model contradicts the prevailing narrative that early societies were dominated by territoriality and rigid social divisions.

Moreover, paleoanthropological discoveries in the African Rift Valley and other significant early human sites reinforce the notion that the earliest Homo sapiens populations thrived through collaboration and the sharing of critical survival knowledge, such as hunting techniques, medicinal plant use, and the creation of communal shelters. The success of these early groups hinged on collective intelligence and solidarity rather than competition and individualism (Aeon, 2018b; MSN, 2021b). Sharing is a practice witnessed in nature across a broad range of organisms, not just humans. Even bears practice sharing when resources are plentiful and bears aren't even social.

In these cultural contexts, the concept of value was deeply embedded in the notion of birthrights—recognizing the communal entitlement to essential resources like water, arable land, shelter, and protection. Such birthrights were not private possessions but communal entitlements that reflected collective stewardship and mutual responsibility (Aeon, 2017a). This worldview prioritized sustaining the group's welfare and future viability over maximizing individual gain.

Importantly, these communal systems had little or no concept of private property, wealth accumulation, or market exchange as understood today. Instead, social cohesion was maintained through informal mechanisms of gifting, sharing, and social reciprocity, which created webs of mutual obligation tying individuals inseparably to their communities (Aeon, 2018a). This dynamic fostered an ethic of generosity and cooperation, reinforcing trust and reducing social inequalities within the group.

Additionally, these early economic arrangements exemplify what some scholars term the gift economy, where circulation of goods and services is governed by social relations and cultural norms rather than monetary calculation. The gift economy is more than an economic system; it is a profound social institution that affirms community, solidarity, and interdependence. The downside, of course, as with all systems, is that Man would never be any better than the system permits. Even supply and demand on such a rudimentary scale will fail in a gifting economy when birthrights are placed at risk. And, 13,000 years ago, that's precisely what happened, leading to the Age of the Swindle with the advent of commonly agreed-upon value economy.

This foundational approach to value was embedded within cosmologies and belief systems that stressed harmony with nature and respect for all living beings. Value was attributed not only to human participants in the economy but extended to the land, animals, and elements, reflecting an integrated ecological consciousness. This orientation contrasts starkly with later ideological shifts that abstract value into quantifiable prices divorced from social and environmental contexts.

Understanding the communal and birthright nature of early value systems sheds critical light on the radical transformations that occurred with the rise of agricultural surpluses, social stratification, and eventually the invention of money. Initially, economy and value were source-dependent. As with all living things capable of the practices, humans had no idea whether and other human valued, or not. Then, the commonly held value emerged and a gifting economic system. These changes introduced fundamentally different conceptions of wealth, property, and exchange that laid the groundwork for contemporary economic ideologies—often at the expense of communal solidarity and egalitarian principles.

By revisiting the roots of value in birthright and shared well-being, we gain valuable insight into alternative models of economic organization that prioritize human dignity, reciprocity, and ecological balance, which sustained our species for 125,000 years and recovered our numbers from no less than three extinction level events during that time. Indeed, from the perspective of unilateral egalitarianism, it was the most successful time in all of human history. Despite the Earth trying to kill us every 50,000 years, or so. Such perspectives challenge dominant assumptions about the inevitability of market capitalism and encourage the exploration of economic systems grounded in community, justice, and sustainable cooperation.

The Shift: Emergence of Surplus and Early Inequality

As human populations grew and societies became more complex, significant transformations in economic and social life took hold, setting the foundation for persistent inequality. The development of agriculture was a pivotal turning point in this process, enabling the production of surplus beyond immediate subsistence needs. Unlike the earlier communal systems tied closely to immediate resource sharing, surplus output could now be stored, accumulated, and—crucially—controlled by individuals or groups. This capacity to produce and hold surplus marked a profound shift in the history of value, initiating a transition from economies based on shared necessity to those structured around accumulation and ownership (Aeon, 2017b). This, then, was the commonly agreed-upon value, monetary economy ideology giving rise to the Age of the Swindle and the system of all human misery.

The emergence of surplus had far-reaching consequences. It enabled new forms of exchange, including long-distance trade, and stimulated the specialization of labor, as not everyone had to be involved directly in food production. Yet, surplus also made possible the concentration of resources in the hands of a few, sowing the seeds for social stratification. Control over stored grain, land, livestock, or crafted goods became a source of power and leverage. Those who controlled the surplus could assert influence over others, not only economically but also politically and culturally. With the emergence of money, everything was given a price tag.

This concentration was bolstered by the establishment of property rights—the conceptual and legal frameworks recognizing exclusive ownership and control over ideas, objects, resources. Property thus transformed from communal stewardship into individualized or elite possession. Alongside this came inheritance laws that formalized the intergenerational transmission of wealth and status, ensuring that privileges and power could be perpetuated over time (Aeon, 2017c). These developments institutionalized inequality by legitimizing the divide between the property-owning elite and the largely dependent masses.

Social hierarchies emerged more distinctly, framed by class distinctions, roles, and often codified in religious or cultural doctrines. Elites justified their privileged positions through ideology – claiming divine sanction, hereditary right, or superior wisdom. These legitimizing narratives served to naturalize inequality and preempt challenges to the emerging order, embedding it deeply within social consciousness.

Concomitant with these changes was the formation of the earliest complex political entities—city-states, kingdoms, and empires—which centralized authority to manage surplus, coordinate large-scale labor, enforce laws, and extract tribute or taxes from the populace (Aeon, 2018c). The state thus became a critical institution for sustaining hierarchical relations. Taxation and tribute systems formalized extraction from common producers, funding elite lifestyles, military enterprises, monumental architecture, and bureaucratic administration.

The institutionalization of surplus control also precipitated shifts in economic relations. Subsistence activities increasingly gave way to market exchanges and tribute-paying obligations. Economic activity became intertwined with political power, as rulers and elites regulated production, distribution, and resource flows. Such control mechanisms diminished the autonomous agency once enjoyed in communal economies, transforming many into subjects dependent on elite redistribution.

Anthropological and archaeological evidence from early civilizations such as Mesopotamia, ancient Egypt, and the Indus Valley demonstrate how temples, palaces, and ruling classes managed surplus collection, storage, and redistribution. These facilities often functioned not only as economic hubs but as centers of ideological control, reinforcing hierarchical social structures through ritual and administration.

Importantly, this shift did not merely reflect material changes but was accompanied by profound transformations in human values and social psychology. The collective ethos of sharing and mutual obligation gave way to norms emphasizing individual entitlement, accumulation, and competition. Values such as generosity and communal welfare were supplanted or subordinated to ideals of possession, legacy, and power.

While surplus production contributed to population growth, technological innovation, and cultural flourishing, it also engendered systemic inequalities—inequalities that persist in evolved forms to the present day. The dawn of property rights, inheritance laws, and institutional hierarchies laid the groundwork for the complex socio-economic stratifications that characterize modern societies.

Understanding this fundamental shift in the conception and management of value is crucial for recognizing the ideological underpinnings of economic inequality. It reveals that property and wealth are not merely neutral facts but are socially constructed mechanisms linked to power, control, and legitimacy. It also underscores the extent to which economic ideologies are embedded in historical contingencies rather than universal necessities.

By tracing the emergence of surplus and early inequality, we gain insight into the origins of divisions that continue to shape human experience—divisions that challenge ideals of justice, cooperation, and shared humanity (Aeon, 2017b; Aeon, 2017c; Aeon, 2018c).

Myth, Metaphor, and the Construction of Value

Throughout history, humans have relied heavily on stories, myths, and metaphors as essential tools to make sense of abstract concepts like value and its distribution. Ancient myths often served to explain the origins of wealth, social order, and political power, as well as to justify existing inequalities. These narratives were not simply fanciful stories but encoded cultural understandings and ethical frameworks that shaped collective behavior and institutional arrangements.

For example, myths surrounding divine right or ancestral blessings provided legitimacy for rulers and elites, presenting wealth and authority as inherently sanctioned and thus unquestionable. Similarly, origin stories about fertile lands or sacred resources grounded a society's relationship to its environment and property norms within cosmological terms that demanded respect and prescribed moral duties. These tales embedded value within a broader context of community, spirituality, and reciprocity rather than reducing it to mere material accumulation.

The metaphors we continue to use today strongly influence not only discourse but also the practical realities of economic life. Metaphors such as the "market" imagined as a living, self-regulating organism, or the "invisible hand" guiding economic outcomes, shape how societies conceptualize economic interactions and human motivations (Aeon, 2018d). These figurative constructs carry powerful normative implications: if the market is seen as an autonomous entity with natural laws, then intervention or redistribution may be viewed as unnatural interference. Likewise, framing economic behaviors as driven by self-interest "invisible hands" can normalize competition and wealth accumulation as virtuous and efficient.

Changing these metaphors can thus have profound ripple effects on social values and institutional practices. When value is metaphorically linked to communal stewardship, sacredness, or lived relationships, societies are more likely to foster norms of sharing, mutual responsibility, and care for collective resources. Such metaphors encourage practices that sustain social bonds and ecological balance. For instance, indigenous and traditional societies often embed economic value within stories that emphasize harmony with nature and interdependence among community members, which in turn guide resource management and social welfare.

Conversely, when metaphors frame value strictly as a commodity to be maximized, bought, or sold, there is a cultural and institutional shift toward competition, individualism, and exploitation (Aeon, 2018d). This shift facilitates the rise of market-centric ideologies, capitalist economies, and consumer cultures where growth and profit become overriding goals—even at the expense of social equity or environmental sustainability. The commodification metaphor abstracts value from relational and ethical contexts, enabling the reduction of people, land, and nature into mere units of exchange.

Moreover, metaphorical language doesn't merely reflect ideology; it actively shapes cognition and decision-making through processes known as conceptual framing. This means that alternative metaphors can open up new ways of thinking and acting. For example, reframing the economy as a "web of life" or a "commons" rather than a "machine" or "market" invites visions of circularity, regeneration, and reciprocity rather than linear extraction and accumulation.

Recognizing the pivotal role of myth and metaphor in constructing value is crucial for efforts aimed at reimagining economic systems. It highlights that ideological transformations require shifts not only in policies and institutions but also in the symbolic frameworks through which societies interpret their world. Changing metaphors can help dissolve rigid ideological patterns and cultivate new collective imaginaries that align more closely with justice, sustainability, and human flourishing.

In this way, the stories we tell—and the metaphors we live by—are not trivial but constitute a fundamental dimension of how value is conceived and enacted socially. They shape our aspirations, fears, and moral commitments, guiding whether societies choose paths of shared prosperity or divisive exploitation.

II. Value: From Birthrights to Commodities

Codification of Value in Ancient Civilizations

With the rise of cities and centralized states, the concept of value underwent profound transformation, becoming increasingly codified and institutionalized in law, custom, and administrative practice. Ancient civilizations such as Mesopotamia, Egypt, the Indus Valley, and early Chinese dynasties developed sophisticated systems to regulate property ownership, inheritance rights, and taxation frameworks that formalized and expanded economic relationships well beyond kinship and communal sharing (Aeon, 2018e).

The advent of writing was a pivotal technological innovation that facilitated this codification. Written records—comprising contracts, ledgers, tax rolls, and legal codes—enabled societies to manage more complex and abstract forms of economic interaction. By recording debts, loans, interest rates, and obligations, ancient administrations established mechanisms for accountability and enforcement previously impossible in oral cultures. These records not only legitimized ownership and transactions but also introduced the legal notion of property as a commodity that could be quantified, transferred, and litigated (Bell et al., 2009).

This shift marked a decisive turn from value as a communal birthright, rooted in shared existence and mutual obligation, to value as a discrete commodity subject to ownership, exchange, and accumulation by individuals or ruling elites. Economic activity increasingly revolved around market-like mechanisms—albeit limited in scope and heavily regulated by political and religious authorities—that commodified land, labor, and goods.

The codification of value underpinned expansionary political ambitions of emerging empires. The aggregation of surplus resources supported larger bureaucracies, standing armies, monumental architecture, and imperial administration. Consequently, forms of exploitation—such as slavery, tributary extraction, and conquest—became institutional cornerstones of power projection and economic control (Aeon, 2017d).

Slavery, in particular, assumed an economic as well as social dimension, with enslaved peoples treated as property that was bought, sold, and deployed for labor exploitation. Tribute systems required subject peoples and conquered territories to provide fixed payments or goods, often exacted through coercion. Such flows enriched central authorities and elites, reinforcing stratification and entrenching inequality.

Legal codes, such as the Code of Hammurabi in Mesopotamia or the Law of the Twelve Tables in Rome, exemplify how the codification of property and value intertwined with social hierarchy. These laws regulated inheritances, property disputes, commercial transactions, and debt obligations, selectively privileging certain classes while constraining others. They helped entrench socioeconomic divides and institutionalized the legitimacy of elite wealth and privilege.

Moreover, the increasing abstraction of value led to early forms of credit and financial instruments that expanded the reach of economic activity but also introduced new vulnerabilities, such as debt peonage and economic dependence. The legal enforcement of debt and interest frequently resulted in the dispossession and subjugation of less powerful groups, reinforcing cycles of poverty and domination.

Religious and ideological frameworks often supported these economic structures by imbuing property rights and social hierarchies with divine sanction. Temples and priestly classes managed vast landholdings and wealth, often acting as economic as well as spiritual centers. The sacralization of wealth and authority masked the constructed nature of economic inequalities and justified systems of exploitation.

Overall, the codification of value in ancient civilizations represents a watershed moment in the history of economic ideology. It marks a transition from embedded, relational economies oriented around birthrights and communal welfare to abstract, institutionalized systems emphasizing individual ownership, exchange, and accumulation. This transformation laid the ideological and material foundations of subsequent economic systems—including feudalism, mercantilism, and capitalism—that continue to shape social relations and global inequalities today.

Understanding this deep historical trajectory is essential for recognizing how economic ideologies are embedded in legal and cultural institutions. It also highlights the ways in which the abstraction and commodification of value serve as instruments of control, producing both economic development and systemic human suffering (Aeon, 2017d; Aeon, 2018e; Bell et al., 2009).

The Invention of Money and the Expansion of Trade

The invention of money represents a crucial turning point in the history of value, profoundly transforming economic and social relations. Prior to money, exchanges were often based on barter systems or reciprocal gifting, which were limited by the need for direct coincidence of wants and tangible relationships. Money, by providing a universal medium of exchange, overcame these limitations and enabled

WORLD PEACE

unprecedented scales of long-distance trade, economic specialization, and market growth (BBC, 2017a).

Money took different forms over time—from early commodity monies such as shells, salt, or cattle, to minted coins, paper notes, and eventually the complex digital currencies we recognize today (Aeon, 2017e). This evolution not only standardized and simplified transactions but also introduced new layers of abstraction in the notion of value. Value became detached from concrete goods or direct social bonds and instead attached to symbolic tokens accepted by collective trust and legal decree.

This abstraction of value brought both innovation and alienation. On one hand, money facilitated complex economic activities such as credit extension, investment, and multi-way trades that expanded capacities for production and exchange. On the other hand, it severed the intimate link between value and social relations, contributing to the commodification of previously non-commercial aspects of life. Land, labor, natural resources, and even human beings became subject to market valuation, trade, and ownership, transforming social and ethical norms profoundly (Glaeser & Scheinkman, 1998).

The accumulation of money enabled the rise of distinct merchant classes and financial intermediaries who specialized in capital circulation, risk management, and profit-making through credit, interest, and speculation. Banking systems emerged to facilitate and regulate these processes, introducing financial instruments such as bills of exchange, bonds, and later, stock markets. These instruments abstracted value further, transforming economic relations into increasingly impersonal, contractual, and speculative forms.

WORLD PEACE

Furthermore, money centralized and intensified economic power, creating new hierarchies and inequalities. Those who controlled capital wielded disproportionate influence over production, political decision-making, and social structures. The ideological narratives surrounding money and markets—such as beliefs in meritocracy, free enterprise, and rational self-interest—were constructed and promoted to legitimize these power dynamics, masking the contingency and constructed nature of economic systems behind claims of natural law and efficiency.

Importantly, money's rise also enabled the commodification of human beings through institutions such as slavery, indentured servitude, and later wage labor systems. Human labor was measured, bought, and sold as a commodity, with profound implications for personal autonomy and social stratification. This commodification underpinned the development of industrial capitalism and global trade networks, linking distant economies into interdependent, but often exploitative, relationships.

The spread of money created incentives for expansionist imperial ventures, as access to bullion, trade routes, and markets became crucial to state power and elite wealth. Colonization and conquest were deeply intertwined with economic imperatives driven by monetary accumulation, often resulting in dispossession, violence, and cultural disruption of indigenous populations.

Despite its enabling role in economic development, money remains a fictional system whose power rests on collective belief, social agreement, and institutional enforcement rather than intrinsic substance. Its symbolic nature means that money can be created, manipulated, and removed under political and social conditions, highlighting its constructed and contingent character.

Understanding money as both a practical tool and an ideological fiction is essential for critiquing the economic inequalities and instabilities that characterize contemporary capitalist societies. This perspective opens pathways to imagining alternative monetary arrangements and economic models that re-embed value in social and ecological contexts, rather than abstract accumulation.

Usury, Debt, and the Moral Economy

As economic systems grew more complex and the circulation of money expanded, societies across different epochs and cultures wrestled with the ethical and moral ramifications of lending, interest, and debt. Usury—the practice of charging interest on loans—was historically condemned by many religious and moral authorities, reflecting profound concerns about the social and spiritual consequences of monetizing credit relationships (Aeon, 2018f). This condemnation was rooted in a broader moral economy that viewed economic transactions as embedded within social obligations and communal welfare, rather than as purely market-driven exchanges (Bell et al., 2009).

In ancient civilizations such as Mesopotamia, Egypt, Greece, and Israel, usury was often linked to exploitation, especially of the poor, farmers, and indebted peasants, who were vulnerable to falling into permanent servitude or losing their land due to unbearable debt burdens. Religious texts—from the Torah and the Bible to early Christian and Islamic teachings—proscribed excessive interest-taking as an affront to justice and charity, advocating mechanisms such as debt forgiveness (e.g., the Jubilee in ancient Israel) to

WORLD PEACE

restore social equilibrium and prevent cycles of dispossession (Aeon, 2018f).

The moral anxiety surrounding usury was thus also an expression of fear about how the abstract power of money could corrode social bonds, converting mutual aid into predatory economic relationships. Debt was understood not merely as a financial instrument but as a potential source of social fracture, hierarchy, and alienation. The role of money was paradoxical—it enabled economic exchange and growth, but its detachment from tangible lives and communities could amplify inequality and undermine communal cohesion.

However, with the rise of commerce, urbanization, and increasingly market-oriented economies during the late medieval and early modern periods, attitudes towards usury gradually shifted. The expansion of trade networks and the emergence of merchant classes required more flexible and formalized credit systems, enabling investment, risk-sharing, and economic expansion. Gradually, many societies relaxed earlier prohibitions, moving toward the legalization and regulation of interest-bearing loans as a practical necessity for economic development (Glaeser & Scheinkman, 1998; Aeon, 2018f).

This transition was not smooth or universal. Intense theological debates raged within Christian Europe, Islamic societies, and elsewhere over the ethics of interest, leading to nuanced doctrinal positions and financial innovations designed to circumvent explicit usury bans. For instance, medieval Christian Europe distinguished between "usury" (excessive interest) and moderate "interest," while Islamic finance developed profit-and-loss sharing contracts as an alternative to interest. These adaptations illustrate how moral constraints were negotiated within evolving economic realities.

Banking institutions and financial markets became engines of capital accumulation and economic growth, channeling resources for trade, infrastructure, and emerging industrial enterprises. Nonetheless, the increased availability of credit also introduced new vulnerabilities. Debt became a double-edged sword: while it catalyzed wealth creation, it also generated systemic risks of overextension, defaults, and crises that reverberated throughout societies.

Periods of financial instability, such as banking collapses, famines triggered by indebted farmers, and popular uprisings against creditors, underscore the persistent tensions embedded in the moral economy of debt. Heavily indebted individuals and communities frequently bore the brunt of exploitation, fueling social unrest and demands for debt relief or reform.

Modern capitalist economies continue to wrestle with the legacies of usury and debt. Consumer credit, mortgage markets, and sovereign debt have become pervasive, raising ethical questions about predatory lending, financialization, and economic sovereignty. The financial crises of recent decades reveal how debt and credit cycles can undermine social stability and exacerbate inequality on a global scale.

Recognizing usury and debt within the moral economy frames these financial instruments not merely as economic tools but as social relations embedded with ethical stakes, power dynamics, and consequences for human dignity and social justice. This perspective calls for critical reflection on how financial systems can be restructured to align economic activity with principles of fairness, responsibility, and communal well-being rather than unchecked profit maximization.

The Cultural Construction of Value

Value is far more than a mere economic metric; it is a deeply rooted cultural construct that permeates religion, philosophy, social norms, and collective narratives. Across societies and historical epochs, the meanings attributed to value shape how resources, labor, and status are understood and distributed, influencing both individual behavior and institutional arrangements.

The cultural construction of value is evident in the stories that the societies demonstrate about wealth, success, and moral worth. For example, in many capitalist societies, the pervasive narrative that "hard work leads to wealth" functions as a legitimizing myth that justifies socioeconomic hierarchies and disparities. This narrative upholds the ideal of meritocracy—the belief that individual effort and talent alone determine economic outcomes—despite extensive sociological and economic research demonstrating the substantial roles of inheritance, systemic bias, and luck in shaping wealth accumulation (Aeon, 2017f; BBC, 2017b). Such dissonance between ideology and empirical reality underscores how cultural stories serve to naturalize specific distributions of wealth and power rather than objectively reflect them.

Religious traditions also contribute significantly to the cultural framing of value. For instance, many Judeo-Christian teachings historically linked wealth to divine favor and poverty to moral failing or testing, embedding economic status within a moral economy that prescribed virtues like charity and temperance alongside reward and punishment

WORLD PEACE

(Bell et al., 2009; Aeon, 2018f). Similarly, other religious and spiritual traditions infuse economic behaviors with sacred meaning, framing value in terms of stewardship, balance, and cosmic order rather than mere accumulation.

Philosophical discourses complement and challenge these cultural valuations. Ethical theories from Aristotle's virtue ethics to modern social contract theory grapple with what constitutes the good life and how societies ought to allocate resources fairly. Yet even within philosophy, varying conceptions of value—from utilitarianism's focus on aggregate welfare to libertarian emphasis on property rights—reflect different underlying cultural assumptions about human nature, freedom, and justice.

Rituals and customs further embody the cultural construction of value. Ceremonies around inheritance, gift-giving, and wealth display communicate and reaffirm social hierarchies and community ties. Laws codify these values by determining rights over property, labor relations, and redistribution, thus institutionalizing specific economic arrangements. For example, inheritance laws often reinforce concentrations of wealth within families or classes, entrenching advantages across generations, while tax codes and social policies reflect collective judgments about fairness and entitlement (Aeon, 2018e; Bell et al., 2009).

Moreover, popular culture and media perpetuate and reshape cultural understandings of value. Advertising, entertainment, and social media platforms often glamorize consumption and wealth accumulation, promoting consumerism as a pathway to happiness and social status. These platforms play active roles in constructing desires and identities around economic success, while sometimes obscuring the structural inequalities and ecological costs embedded in such models (Davidow, 2021).

The cultural construction of value is neither immutable nor uniform. It is subject to contestation, reinterpretation, and change as societies evolve. Social movements challenging injustice, poverty, and environmental degradation often question dominant value narratives, proposing alternative frameworks that emphasize equity, sustainability, and collective well-being. Such efforts highlight how cultural meanings of value are central to political struggles over resource distribution and social justice.

Understanding value as a cultural construction rather than an objective fact is essential for critically engaging with economic systems and their impacts. It reveals that what societies prize—and how they justify inequalities—depends on shared meanings and power relations embedded in culture. This awareness opens possibilities for reimagining value in ways that align more closely with human dignity, ecological integrity, and social solidarity.

III. Economy: From Communal Systems to Capitalist Structures

The Rise of Capitalism

The emergence of capitalism in early modern Europe marked a profound and transformative shift in the history of value and economic organization. Capitalism is fundamentally defined by private ownership of the means of production, the employment of wage labor, and the pursuit of profit primarily through market exchange mechanisms (Wikipedia, n.d.-a). This system replaced earlier communal and feudal economic forms, unleashing unprecedented levels of economic growth, technological innovation, and productivity. However, this progress came with significant social and environmental costs, deepening divisions within society, entrenching inequality, and contributing to ecological degradation (Britannica, n.d.).

Historically, the roots of capitalism can be traced back to the late Middle Ages and Renaissance periods in Europe, especially within the competitive Italian city-states such as Florence, Venice, and Genoa. These regions pioneered financial innovations like bills of exchange and banking practices, facilitating long-distance trade and capital accumulation. The expansion of commerce, the growth of markets, and the consolidation of strong nation-states through mercantilism laid the institutional groundwork for the broader capitalist development that spread across Europe during the 16th to 18th centuries (Wikipedia, n.d.-a; Britannica, n.d.).

One of the defining features of capitalist economies is competition, which operates as a driving force for increasing efficiency, reducing costs, and fostering innovation. Firms and individuals are motivated to innovate and improve their production to maximize profits and capture greater market share. While this competitive dynamic has fueled technological advancements and economic development, it also creates cyclical patterns characterized by booms and busts that contribute to economic instability and recurrent crises (Aeon, 2018g).

Another central characteristic of capitalism is commodification. In capitalist economies, goods, services, and even social relations become commodities—objects that can be bought, sold, and valued in monetary terms. This commodification extends beyond tangible products to include labor, natural resources, and cultural elements. As a result, social interactions are increasingly mediated through market mechanisms rather than communal or relational considerations (Aeon, 2018h).

Despite contributing to overall increases in wealth and standards of living in many regions, capitalism inherently tends to concentrate wealth and power in the hands of a relatively small elite. Persistent disparities between rich and poor remain a hallmark of capitalist societies, with recent data indicating rising income inequality in numerous countries. These disparities raise concerns about social cohesion, equitable opportunity, and the long-term stability of societies (World Bank, 2024; UN World Social Report 2025).

Capitalism is also characterized by globalization, where modern capitalist economies are deeply interconnected through global trade, financial flows, and migration. This integration spreads both economic prosperity and precarity around the world, creating complex dependencies. While wealthier countries often benefit disproportionately, vulnerable populations may suffer from exploitation, job displacement, and environmental harm. The rapid dissemination of technology and knowledge enhances global economic integration but simultaneously fuels social tensions and backlash in affected communities (BBC, 2017c; BBC News, 2016).

Critiques of capitalism emphasize its tendencies to generate class conflict, foster cronyism and corruption, produce environmental externalities such as pollution and resource depletion, and perpetuate systemic social inequalities. In response, there are growing calls for reforms aimed at promoting sustainability and equity. These include movements toward stakeholder capitalism, corporate social responsibility, and regulatory frameworks that internalize environmental and social costs. However, such approaches face significant challenges in balancing profit motives with ecological and social goals (Investopedia, 2025; Britannica, 2025; IMF, 2024).

More recent developments such as eco-capitalism and sustainable capitalism seek to integrate ecological concerns and social governance into capitalist frameworks. These paradigms aim to mitigate capitalism's negative externalities and foster long-term planetary and human welfare. While promising, they must grapple with the fundamental tension between profit-driven motives and sustainability imperatives (Wikipedia, 2001).

In summary, the rise of capitalism represents a complex historical evolution marked by both remarkable economic dynamism and profound social and environmental challenges. Understanding capitalism's multifaceted impacts is essential for engaging in informed discussions about how economic systems might be reformed or transformed to better serve the future of humanity and the planet.

The Ideology of Economic Growth

The ideology of economic growth has become an almost unquestioned central tenet of modern societies, deeply embedded within political agendas, media discourse, and public consciousness. Gross Domestic Product (GDP), stock market indices, and productivity statistics serve as primary metrics for assessing a country's success and progress, often overshadowing more holistic considerations of human well-being, social equity, and ecological sustainability (BBC,

WORLD PEACE

2017d). This dominant focus privileges continuous quantitative expansion of economic output as the ultimate societal objective, framing growth not merely as desirable but as essential for maintaining social order and prosperity.

Rooted in Enlightenment-era conceptions of progress and further entrenched by post-World War II development paradigms, the growth ideology assumes that increases in material production and consumption naturally translate into improved living standards for all. However, this assumption masks significant trade-offs and distributive conflicts inherent in growth-centered policies. The relentless pursuit of GDP growth can generate environmental degradation on an unprecedented scale, including deforestation, biodiversity loss, climate change, and pollution of air, water, and soil. These ecological costs often disproportionately affect marginalized communities, exacerbating social dislocation and inequality (Aeon, 2018i).

Moreover, economic growth as a singular focus frequently erodes traditional ways of life and cultural practices, especially those grounded in communal values and sustainable resource use. Globalization and market integration driven by growth imperatives accelerate homogenization of cultures and disrupt local economies and social fabrics. This can lead to alienation, loss of identity, and social fragmentation, further undermining community resilience and well-being.

The ideology also shapes policy priorities, incentivizing governments to favor industries and sectors that maximize output and financial returns rather than those that promote health, education, environmental stewardship, or social welfare. Infrastructure projects, technological innovation, and trade liberalization are often pursued with GDP

Burl Minnis

WORLD PEACE

enhancement as the primary justification, while externalities—such as environmental damage or social displacement—are undervalued or ignored. Such policies may consolidate power within elite economic actors and corporations capable of capitalizing on growth opportunities, while bypassing broader participatory governance and accountability.

Critically, alternative approaches that emphasize sustainability, equity, and quality of life—such as the concept of "steady-state" or "degrowth" economies—are frequently marginalized or dismissed within dominant discourse. These perspectives challenge the premise that infinite growth is compatible with finite planetary boundaries and urge a reevaluation of what constitutes genuine prosperity. Similarly, measures of well-being beyond GDP, such as the Human Development Index, Genuine Progress Indicator, or social and environmental accounting frameworks, remain secondary in policy considerations despite their more comprehensive nature.

The economic growth ideology thus sustains a narrative where perpetual expansion is equated with human progress, often at the expense of ecological and social health. Its persistence is reinforced by vested interests, institutional inertia, and cognitive biases favoring material accumulation and short-term gains.

Understanding the ideological underpinnings of economic growth is crucial for imagining and advancing more just, resilient, and sustainable futures. It calls for integrating environmental limits, social justice, and cultural diversity into economic decision-making and embracing pluralistic measures of success that transcend mere numerical growth (BBC, 2017d; Aeon, 2018i).

WORLD PEACE

The Consequences: War, Poverty, and Systemic Suffering

The consequences of economic ideology are starkly visible in the persistence of war, poverty, and systemic suffering across the globe. Economic interests have historically played a determinative role in driving conflicts, colonialism, and imperial expansion. Countries and corporations alike, motivated by the pursuit of control over valuable resources, strategic markets, and exploitable labor pools, have often instigated or perpetuated violent confrontations to secure advantageous positions within the global economic order (Aeon, 2018j). This logic of economic conquest has justified widespread exploitation, large-scale displacement of populations, and brutal violence that reverberates through generations (Aeon, 2018k).

These economic motivations are intricately linked to geopolitical ambitions, where rivalry over oil, minerals, arable land, and trade routes fuels proxy wars, military interventions, and the militarization of borders. The consequences are not limited to battlefield deaths alone but also include the destruction of infrastructure, environmental degradation, and the fracturing of social fabrics essential for community resilience. Corporate actors often benefit from these conditions, profiting from resource extraction, arms sales, and reconstruction contracts, entrenching cycles of conflict and inequality.

Even as global wealth has increased in aggregate terms, these gains have been uneven and insufficient to eradicate poverty. Vast populations remain trapped in conditions of deprivation, lacking access to basic necessities such as clean water, healthcare, education, and stable employment. The persistence, and in many regions, intensification of

WORLD PEACE

inequality signal systemic failures in how economic benefits are distributed. Capital accumulation typically concentrates wealth within a small elite, who influence policy to preserve their interests, often at the expense of marginalized and vulnerable groups (World Bank, 2024; Aeon, 2018l).

Economic policies driven by neoliberal ideology—commonly characterized by austerity measures, deregulation of markets, and privatization of public services—have exacerbated hardships for many. Austerity often leads to cuts in social safety nets, healthcare, and education, disproportionately impacting the poor and widening inequalities. Deregulation can weaken labor protections and environmental standards, allowing exploitative practices to flourish. Privatization shifts essential services from public accountability to profit-driven entities, frequently resulting in reduced access and affordability for those who need them most. Such policies can provoke social unrest, protests, and undermine democratic governance, as citizens bear the brunt of economic restructuring that prioritizes market efficiency over human dignity.

Furthermore, cycles of debt—both at the level of individuals and countries—trap countless communities in chronic insecurity. Structural adjustment programs imposed by international financial institutions often compel indebted countries to adopt policies that prioritize debt repayment over social investments, deepening poverty and social dislocation. On an individual level, unemployment, precarious work, and lack of social protections foster environments of marginalization where opportunities for economic mobility are severely limited. These intertwined crises of debt and labor exclusion perpetuate conditions where entire populations face food insecurity, inadequate housing, and poor health outcomes, exacerbating social fragmentation and vulnerability.

The systemic nature of suffering under dominant economic ideologies reveals that poverty and conflict are not accidental byproducts but embedded features of the global economic system. They arise from structural inequalities reinforced by legal, financial, and institutional frameworks that govern production, trade, and resource allocation. Breaking these cycles requires not only addressing immediate material conditions but also challenging the ideological assumptions that naturalize profit maximization and growth as overriding imperatives.

Efforts to mitigate these consequences increasingly emphasize the importance of inclusive development models, fair trade principles, debt relief initiatives, and the strengthening of human rights protections. Social movements worldwide advocate for more equitable economic systems that center the needs and dignity of people rather than the interests of capital. Environmental justice campaigns highlight the interconnectedness of ecological sustainability and social well-being, underscoring that long-term solutions must integrate these dimensions.

Understanding the deep interconnections between economic ideology, war, poverty, and systemic suffering is thus essential for imagining and actualizing alternative futures. Such futures prioritize justice, equity, and peace over accumulation and domination, acknowledging the shared humanity and dignity of all individuals affected by these entrenched systems.

WORLD PEACE

Economic Crises and the Limits of Growth

The history of the modern economy is marked by recurring and often devastating crises—financial panics, recessions, depressions, and speculative bubbles—that repeatedly expose the vulnerabilities of prevailing economic systems. From early episodes like the Dutch Tulip Mania in the 17th century, which epitomized the irrational exuberance and speculative excess of asset bubbles, to the catastrophic Great Depression of the 1930s, the 2008 global financial crisis, and the more recent volatility witnessed in cryptocurrency markets, these crises have illustrated the persistent fragility underlying systems that place growth and profit above all other considerations (Wikipedia, n.d.-b; BBC, 2017e).

These upheavals are not mere accidents or anomalies but symptomatic of deeper structural flaws in economic models that relentlessly prioritize quantitative expansion, often neglecting the social and ecological costs of such growth. The systemic risks embedded within financial markets—including excessive leverage, speculative trading, and opaque derivative instruments—are exacerbated by deregulation trends that reduce oversight and increase volatility. Deregulation, touted as a means to unleash market efficiency, has at times facilitated reckless behaviors and the concentration of financial power, reducing transparency and accountability (Aeon, 2018m).

Moreover, economic crises highlight the dangerous consequences of excessive financialization, whereby economic activity becomes dominated more by speculative financial transactions than by productive investments in goods and services. This shift undermines the real economy by detaching capital flows from tangible production and community welfare, fostering bubbles that inflate and burst with destructive consequences for employment, social stability, and public trust.

The erosion of social safety nets further compounds the human costs of economic downturns. Cuts to welfare programs, unemployment benefits, and public health systems—often implemented in the name of fiscal austerity—leave vulnerable populations exposed to heightened insecurity during times of crisis. This amplification of inequality and precarity weakens social cohesion, fueling political instability and undermining democratic institutions.

Repeated crises also expose the limitations of traditional economic growth paradigms, which assume continuous expansion is both feasible and universally beneficial. Yet, ecological constraints and finite resource availability challenge the sustainability of perpetual growth models. The pursuit of ever-higher GDP figures ignores environmental degradation, climate change impacts, and biodiversity loss, issues that increasingly precipitate economic shocks themselves through disasters, supply chain disruptions, and resource scarcity.

These systemic vulnerabilities necessitate a critical reassessment of the growth-centric ideology that dominates mainstream economics and policy. Alternative approaches advocate for resilient and equitable economic systems that prioritize stability, sustainability, and human well-being over mere accumulation of wealth. Concepts such as "degrowth," "steady-state economics," and "circular economies" emphasize the need to balance economic activity within planetary boundaries while ensuring social justice and quality of life.

In essence, economic crises reveal the brittle foundations of systems that subordinate social and ecological imperatives to financial profit and expansion. They underscore the urgent need to integrate regulatory frameworks that promote transparency, accountability, and risk mitigation alongside robust social protections. Without such reforms, history suggests that economic instability and its attendant social harms will persist as defining features of global capitalism.

Recognizing the limits of growth is not merely an economic imperative but a moral one, inviting societies to reconsider values, metrics of success, and long-term goals in crafting sustainable and just futures (Aeon, 2018m; Wikipedia, n.d.-b; BBC, 2017e).

The Role of Theory and the Dangers of Abstraction

Economics as a discipline has long depended on abstract models and formal mathematical theories to explain and predict human behavior within markets and societies. These models seek to simplify complex reality by isolating key variables and relationships, allowing economists to formulate generalized principles and testable hypotheses. While such theoretical frameworks can provide valuable insights into economic mechanisms, systemic patterns, and potential policy outcomes, this reliance on abstraction carries significant risks and limitations (Aeon, 2018n).

One major danger of overreliance on abstract models is that they often fail to capture the multifaceted and context-dependent nature of real-world economic phenomena. Economic behavior is embedded in cultural, social, historical, and political contexts that shape decision-making and resource allocation in ways that simple models may overlook or oversimplify. For instance, assumptions of

WORLD PEACE

rational actors optimizing utility under perfect information rarely hold true in everyday life, where individuals face uncertainty, bounded rationality, and complex social influences. Ignoring these nuances can lead to models that are elegant on paper but disconnected from lived experience and practical realities (Aeon, 2018n).

Moreover, the abstraction inherent in economic theory can obscure critical aspects of value that are not easily quantifiable—such as ethical considerations, social justice, environmental sustainability, and human well-being. By focusing primarily on measurable metrics such as prices, outputs, and efficiencies, economic models may sideline or discount factors that carry profound significance for communities and ecosystems. This can result in policy prescriptions that optimize narrow economic goals while exacerbating inequalities, damaging environments, or undermining social cohesion.

The consequences of this disconnect are evident in instances where economic theories have guided policy decisions that ultimately failed to anticipate or adequately respond to crises. The 2008 financial collapse, for example, exposed the shortcomings of prevailing macroeconomic models that underestimated systemic risk and financial contagion. Similarly, austerity measures implemented based on certain economic doctrines led to widespread social hardship and political instability in various countries, highlighting how theoretical frameworks divorced from social realities can cause harm when applied rigidly (Aeon, 2018o).

Overemphasis on abstraction also risks creating an exclusive technical language and institutional culture that alienates the public and marginalizes alternative perspectives rooted in lived experience and interdisciplinary approaches. This can foster a sense of economic expertise as disconnected or inaccessible, weakening democratic deliberation about economic policies and their broader societal implications.

To address these challenges, there is growing recognition within the field of economics of the need for pluralism— embracing diverse methodologies, qualitative insights, and critical reflection on the assumptions underlying models. Incorporating perspectives from behavioral economics, economic anthropology, political economy, and ecological economics enriches understanding by situating economic activity within its wider social and environmental contexts.

Furthermore, integrating empirical observation with theory in a dialectical manner enhances the relevance and responsiveness of economic knowledge. This approach respects the complexity and dynamism of human economies, acknowledging uncertainty, feedback loops, and value pluralism.

By remaining critically aware of the limits of abstraction and striving for models that are not only analytically rigorous but also contextually grounded and ethically informed, economics can contribute more effectively to policies that promote equitable, sustainable, and humane economies.

In summary, while economic theory offers indispensable tools for understanding and managing economic systems, overreliance on abstract models risks oversimplification, policy blindness, and social disconnection. A balanced approach that integrates theory with real-world complexity and ethical sensitivity is essential for reimagining value and economy in ways that align with the needs and dignity of all people and the planet (Aeon, 2018n; Aeon, 2018o).

Conclusion

The history of value and the economy is fundamentally a story of profound transformation. It charts humanity's journey from early communal systems based on birthrights and reciprocal relations, characterized by cooperation and shared stewardship, to increasingly commodified arrangements where goods, land, labor, and even social relations are bought, sold, and quantified in market terms. This trajectory reflects a shift from moral economies—where economic activity was embedded within social, ethical, and ecological contexts—to disembedded, profit-driven systems that prioritize accumulation, competition, and growth above all else (Aeon, 2018a; Aeon, 2017a; Aeon, 2017b).

While such developments have undeniably facilitated remarkable technological innovation, increased productivity, and the expansion of human capability on an unprecedented scale, they have also brought about deep and persistent inequalities. The codification of property, the institutionalization of inheritance and debt, and the emergence of money transformed economic relations in ways that concentrated power and wealth, enabling systems of exploitation that have caused and perpetuated widespread poverty, social dislocation, and systemic suffering (Aeon, 2018e; Bell et al., 2009; World Bank, 2024). Economic ideologies have supported and justified colonialism, slavery, imperial conquest, and environmental degradation, often cloaked in narratives of progress, merit, and natural order, masking the constructed nature and consequences of these systems (Aeon, 2017d; Aeon, 2018j; Aeon, 2018k).

The recurring cycles of economic crises—from historic financial panics to modern recessions and speculative

WORLD PEACE

bubbles—along with the erosion of social safety nets and deepening global disparities, underscore the limitations and dangers inherent in current growth- and profit-centered economic paradigms (Wikipedia, n.d.-b; BBC, 2017e; Aeon, 2018m; World Bank, 2024). Furthermore, the dominant reliance on abstract economic models and theories has often failed to account adequately for complex social realities, ethical considerations, and ecological constraints, leading to policy failures and disconnection from lived experience (Aeon, 2018n; Aeon, 2018o).

Amidst these challenges, there is growing recognition of the need to rethink value and economy fundamentally. Alternative models—such as the revival of gift economies and commons-based stewardship, the development of social and solidarity economies, and the radical proposals of degrowth and post-growth—offer hopeful pathways that reconnect economic activity with human dignity, social justice, and ecological sustainability (Aeon, 2018p; Aeon, 2018q; Aeon, 2018r). These models draw both on ancient wisdom and contemporary innovations to envision economic systems rooted not in abstraction and accumulation, but in cooperation, democratic participation, and respect for the interconnectedness of human and nonhuman life.

Looking forward, the accelerating technological transformations of the digital age pose both unprecedented opportunities and complex ethical dilemmas. Emerging forms of value creation through digital platforms, cryptocurrencies, and decentralized finance challenge existing institutional arrangements, even as issues of privacy, surveillance, algorithmic bias, and exacerbated inequalities raise pressing questions about justice and governance (BBC, 2017f; CNN, 2017; Aeon, 2018s; World

WORLD PEACE

Bank, 2024). Navigating these challenges demands thoughtful integration of technological innovation with ethical frameworks and inclusive policies that ensure equitable benefit sharing and protect fundamental rights.

Central to this reimagining of value and economy is education, and particularly the cultivation of critical economic literacy. By equipping individuals with the knowledge and analytical skills to understand, critique, and engage with dominant economic ideologies and alternative paradigms, education becomes a crucial driver of democratic participation and social transformation (Aeon, 2018t). It enables people to actively participate in shaping economic systems aligned with justice, sustainability, and collective well-being.

Ultimately, understanding the historical evolution of value and economy reveals that prevailing systems are neither natural nor inevitable but contingent and constructed. This insight empowers the possibility and responsibility to forge economic futures that learn from past mistakes and embrace human and ecological flourishing. The work ahead involves dismantling entrenched injustices, reweaving social and ecological relations, and cultivating virtues such as empathy, integrity, and courage that align with reasoned principles (Oxford Academic, n.d.; Aeon, n.d.).

By advancing these transformative visions, humanity can aspire toward more just, equitable, and sustainable societies—where economic systems serve life rather than undermine it, and where the lessons of history fuel hope and collective action for a better future. Abolishing money does not mean the absence of economy, nor any of the aforementioned principles and properties of economy. Rather, the currency of capitalism, or socialism, or any of a number of economic systems today, becomes doing the needful thing.

Doing the needful things becomes the only currency of any value in all matters, returning the focus to the laborer, simultaneously promoting human resource meritocracy and generalization of skillsets, just from a change in the currency. But the absence of the money keystone further ensures a large and mobile workforce to undertaker those needful things worldwide honorably, nobly, in the efforts of our redemption as a species. Without money standing in the way, success in our endeavors is assured.

Truly, nothing changes for Man in the absence of money, except that Man is once again in charge as a rational reasonable actor. As such, current principles and properties of economic systems, afore described, are made more amenable for all life on Earth, simply by the virtues of Man serving as the economic driver. Without the influence of toxins and maladies, Man becomes free—free to achieve sustainability of resources, free to attain unilateral egalitarianism worldwide, free to enjoy equity among the siblings from the last iteration in the family of Man. Together.

WORLD PEACE

Chapter 5: The Illusion of Hardship and the Role of the Messenger
Life is Never Hard

The widespread belief that life must inherently be hard or that suffering is an unavoidable and integral feature of human existence is not necessarily a reflection of innate human nature. Instead, it is more accurately understood as a complex product shaped and reinforced by layered social constructs that have evolved over time. We moved away from the life of bonobos and adopted the ways of chimpanzees. Anthropological and historical research reveals that throughout numerous cultures and epochs, humans have found ways to flourish by establishing systems grounded not in competition and enforced scarcity but in cooperation, reciprocal sharing, and mutual aid—fundamental principles that have historically sustained communities and fostered well-being (Aeon, 2017a; Yeston et al., 2006).

Many of the social and economic frameworks that promote the idea of relentless struggle as a natural or even virtuous condition often serve interests that are far narrower than the collective common good. For example, consider the practice of "de-banking"—a process whereby individuals or entire communities are excluded from access to the formal banking system. De-banking is not an unavoidable economic reality but a deliberate artifact shaped by policy decisions, regulatory frameworks, and prevailing ideological commitments that prioritize particular power structures over equitable access (Wikipedia, n.d.a). In this context, the commonplace acceptance of poverty and precarity as inevitable consequences of absolute resource scarcity has been repeatedly challenged and debunked. Instead, these

WORLD PEACE

adverse conditions frequently stem from intentional policy choices and economic arrangements architected to create distinct winners and losers within society (Aeon, 2017b; The Real News, 2018). I'm sure everyone in the US, at least, remembers the practice of "redlining".

Contemporary capitalism, scrutinized extensively by scholars such as Streeck (2017), has gradually evolved into a system that normalizes and perpetuates profound inequality under the veneer of progress and meritocracy. Within this paradigm, workers are often socially and culturally conditioned to find existential purpose predominantly through labor, as corporate entities appropriate idealistic language—traditionally associated with community and personal fulfillment—for the pursuit of profit maximization. This occurs even as CEO compensation continues to escalate exponentially, creating an ever-widening chasm between top executives and average workers, further entrenching systemic disparity (BBC, 2017; The Real News, 2017a). Such dominant narratives obscure and divert attention away from the transformative potential of scientific and technological advances. For instance, revolutionary medical innovations like the first approved "living drug" for cancer treatment (Gallagher, 2017) hold the promise to drastically alleviate human suffering on a large scale. Yet, access to such breakthroughs remains severely constrained by profit-driven frameworks that place economic returns above equitable distribution.

Historical insights offer compelling critiques of the assumed naturalness of hardship and competition. The classic board game Monopoly—originally conceptualized as a critique to expose the dangers inherent in unrestrained capitalism—has paradoxically become a widely accepted model of economic competition in mainstream popular culture (Aeon, 2015a).

Burl Minnis

WORLD PEACE

This exemplifies how public perception can be subtly shaped to accept the privatization of essential resources, such as water, as inevitable or even desirable. Periodic, temporary reversals in these privatization policies are often heralded as significant victories, though they rarely challenge the underlying commodification logic that promotes resource exclusion and inequality (The Real News, 2019).

Furthermore, the availability of fundamental necessities is frequently complicated by artificial scarcity deliberately engineered through so-called "market solutions." These solutions maintain uneven access and privilege a narrow subset of individuals or corporations, resulting in widespread deprivation despite abundant resources (Aeon, 2017b). These artificially induced constraints are compounded by the proliferation of technical economic jargon that has, in many instances, served to normalize and legitimize these constraints, thereby making their existence seem natural, rational, or immutable (Aeon, 2015b).

Modern societal messaging often conflates overwork and perpetual labor with virtue and personal meaning, persuading the public that fulfillment is achievable only through participation in institutionalized labor systems. This juxtaposition occurs even as systemic inequality deepens, masking structural injustices and perpetuating a cycle of exploitation (BBC, 2017; The Real News, 2017a). Importantly, this widespread acceptance of hardship as an intrinsic aspect of life is neither biologically predetermined nor inevitable; instead, it is a historically constructed ideology that serves to maintain existing power dynamics (Streeck, 2017).

In addition to these ideological barriers, tangible social and scientific innovations with demonstrated capacity to radically reduce human suffering—ranging from government-backed food assistance programs (Aeon, 2016b), collaborative community action initiatives, to cutting-edge health interventions (Gallagher, 2017; PBS, 2017)—are often constrained and limited by bureaucratic inertia, monetary priorities, and ideological boundaries. These constraints prevent or delay their broad implementation, underscoring that the notion of life's inherent hardness is as much an artifact of human policy and belief systems as it is a product of objective reality.

The Psychology of Manufactured Hardship

Scarcity thinking—the pervasive belief that resources are intrinsically limited and that hardship is inevitable—is not a natural or objective fact, but rather a socially constructed narrative perpetuated because it serves the interests of certain powerful groups. This mindset has been deliberately embedded into public consciousness because it benefits some actors economically, while simultaneously pacifying others by normalizing struggle and limiting aspirations (The Real News, 2018; Aeon, 2017c). The widespread prevalence of high costs for basic human needs, persistent financial insecurity among large segments of the population, and the systemic normalization of precarious labor conditions are not outcomes dictated by immutable natural laws or unavoidable market forces. Instead, they are direct consequences of explicit policy decisions and strategic choices made by policymakers, corporate executives, and financial institutions which shape the rules and frameworks within which economic life unfolds as humans participate without option to do so. We could keep applying Band-Aids to the symptoms of the problem and never move closer to world peace. But if we abolish the true problem – money –

WORLD PEACE

no Band-Aids would be needed, and world peace could exist in its entirety.

At the structural level, many economic systems are designed such that the burden of hardship, risk, and failure is disproportionately shifted onto individuals and families. Meanwhile, the broader systemic arrangements— governments, corporations, and financial markets—remain largely insulated from direct accountability or critique. This asymmetry is glaringly evident in areas such as healthcare. Take, for instance, the institutionalized practice of medical abandonment of hospice patients, where end-of-life care is often managed so impersonally and bureaucratically that it becomes an individual problem to bear, rather than recognized and addressed as a collective societal responsibility (PBS, 2017). This bureaucratic framing, centered on cost-cutting and administrative efficiency, neglects the profound communal and relational dimensions intrinsic to compassionate care.

By reframing care not as an isolated burden placed on individuals and their families but as a shared communal responsibility embedded within social infrastructure, we could radically transform the experience of hardship, especially for the most vulnerable populations. Historical and anthropological evidence demonstrates that many societies thrived for centuries through systems based on cooperation, mutual aid, and shared risk management, rather than competitive individualism (Yeston et al., 2006). Such collective approaches to care and resource distribution offer pathways to mitigate manufactured hardship and foster resilience, reducing the psychological as well as material toll that scarcity thinking imposes on society at large. Eliminate money, and anyone could earn a medical degree. Life doesn't need to be this hard.

WORLD PEACE

Erasing the Myth of Inescapable Difficulty

The widespread view that hardship and suffering are immutable, inherent aspects of human life—an inexorable "just how life is" condition—overlooks rich and diverse social practices that have historically minimized such difficulties. Long before modern economic systems dominated by profit motives, many societies functioned through gift economies and entrenched traditions of mutual care, cooperation, and reciprocal support, which effectively served to buffer individuals and communities from extreme suffering and deprivation (Aeon, 2018b; Aeon, 2016a). These modes of economic and social organization prioritized human need, social cohesion, and shared well-being over competitive accumulation or centralized control.

Intriguingly, recent research into the origins of writing challenges conventional assumptions that it emerged primarily as a tool for bureaucratic accounting or commodification. Instead, evidence suggests that the earliest systems of writing and record-keeping were often developed as instruments for fostering social hopes, dreams, religious aspirations, and community cohesion. These systems aimed to strengthen trust and collective identity rather than simply monitoring exchanges for economic gain (Aeon, 2016a).

When examining the genuine historical record in its entirety, a consistent pattern emerges: communities and societies that place human needs and collective achievement at their center have successfully diminished hardship and elevated well-being across generations. Such societies resisted the forces of commodification and hierarchical control that tend to exacerbate inequality and suffering. In contrast, systemic structures undergirded by profit, competition, and exclusion often generate cycles of hardship that are neither natural nor unavoidable but rather socially engineered results of those priorities (Streeck, 2017). These findings make it clear that suffering is not an inevitable destiny for humankind; rather, it is significantly a legacy—often a deliberate consequence—of political and economic systems that prioritize interests other than the collective thriving of human communities (Aeon, 2015b; The Real News, 2018). The price of freedom is not high. It is always free. The price of ideology is what costs us to death.

Messenger and Message: Social Dynamics

Individuals who act as the voice for the majority of rational human actors often find themselves vilified, marginalized, or outright dismissed—not because their accounts lack accuracy or validity, but because their revelations disrupt entrenched balances of comfort, power, and control within society. The dynamic of vilification serves to protect established interests by maintaining the status quo and discouraging critical inquiry into deeply held beliefs and systems of authority (Aeon, 2017d). This pattern of resistance toward messengers recurs consistently across history, social movements, and cultural productions, which seek to emancipate the public from socially constructed inevitabilities by critically interrogating and exposing the fictions underpinning economic, political, and social practices (Joseph, 2007; Joseph, 2008; Joseph, 2011).

Extensive social research and philosophical analyses emphasize that the disruptive nature of the messenger's work comes precisely from their role in unearthing uncomfortable facts and challenging seeming certainties. By exposing suffering, inequality, and social dysfunction as not immutable or predetermined, but rather as contingent on specific social, economic, and political arrangements, these messengers reveal that these conditions are in fact mutable and subject to conscious, collective human will and intervention (Aeon, 2017d; Streeck, 2017).

Recent advancements in genetics and anthropology further complicate simplistic and essentialist narratives about human origins and identity. Emerging evidence from these disciplines continually reshapes our understanding of what it means to be human, debunking mainstream stories that have historically presented a linear, homogeneous view of human development. Instead, these studies highlight the diverse, contingent, and evolving nature of human ancestry and cultural identity—showing that received narratives have always been partial and subject to revision as new discoveries are made (NPR, 2020; Smithsonian Magazine, 2020). This reinforces the critical insight that many social constructs we accept as fixed reality are, instead, contingent fictions open to transformation. Regardless, fiction cannot influence reality with any measure of success, and the only evidence we have for that assertion is that no ideology has ever solved anything. And, whenever either economy, or politics ideology fails, it murders millions, worldwide.

Systemic Inertia and Collective Responsibility

Modern societies are increasingly characterized by pervasive systems of surveillance, data collection, and manipulation that extend deeply into everyday life. From large-scale data exploitation scandals revealing the unauthorized harvesting and commodification of personal information (Wikipedia, n.d.c; ICIJ, 2021), to the widespread privatization and commodification of knowledge, these systems reveal a deliberate architecture designed to consolidate and perpetuate existing power

WORLD PEACE

structures (Zuboff, 2019; Aeon, 2020). While technological and scientific advancements possess the extraordinary potential to alleviate countless forms of human hardship—improving health, increasing productivity, and expanding access to resources—their deployment is frequently co-opted to sharpen social and economic inequalities. Technologies become tools not just of progress but of control: monitoring marginalized populations, intensifying labor demands, and embedding disenfranchisement within digital infrastructures (Aeon, 2019).

Those who serve as messengers, today, (which will include you with your contribution, in essence) regarding this particular mission of the majority, face the imperative to expose not only the immediate, visible hardships experienced by individuals and communities but also to reveal the underlying systemic mechanisms that obscure and naturalize such suffering as a permanent fixture of life. That's precisely what Article 15 of the Rome Statute is for. The POICC website has a full set of instructions on how to submit claims and evidence, and your contribution is no different.

Organized, and/or institutionalized ideology is a conative toxin in Man, bringing about human extinction. As such, continued practice is deemed a crime against humanity, and will desist immediately. Get on your emergency broadcasting systems, worldwide, and announce; set all general ledgers and abolish money as the keystone of all human misery. We're never going back. Practically a bumper sticker slogan in its simplicity. This demystification process works against the normalization of inequality and hardship by unveiling how much of what appears inevitable is, in fact, engineered and maintained by intentional policies, economic incentives, and ideological narratives.

Consequently, what is urgently required is a persistent, collective skepticism toward prevailing narratives that present hardship as an inescapable destiny. So, contribute your voice to the POICC as a member of the majority. History reminds us that transformative change has never emerged from fatalistic resignation or passivity. The historical figures who reshaped societies—abolitionists who dismantled slavery, visionaries who championed civil rights, and defenders who protected the vulnerable—did not craft utopias from thin air. Rather, their profound impact arose from the steadfast insistence that existing conditions were not fixed or universal but contingent and changeable. They drew strength and inspiration from concrete examples elsewhere and built movements grounded in the belief that better ways of living and relating were possible and already in practice (Aeon, 2017e). This collective responsibility to critically question, resist, and transform injustice remains the foundation for any genuine progress toward a more equitable and compassionate world. Contribute your voice. Be a part of this moment in human history. Join the majority for the big win of rational reasonable right action. It's just a letter writing campaign.

Life Reimagined: If Not Hard, Then What?

The rejection of hardship as an unavoidable, fixed feature of human existence does not imply the promise of a flawless utopia. Rather, it requires considerable courage and critical insight: the willingness to recognize that much of the suffering we endure is not a natural given but frequently artificial, socially constructed, and deliberately engineered through political, economic, and ideological mechanisms (Streeck, 2017). Humans everywhere do not hate humans everywhere else, for instance. Even the suggestion of such a thing is counterintuitive since humans do not know all other humans. And, we already know that anything counterintuitive to a human means a swindle is at hand. That's political ideology nonsense. It's not intended to make sense; it's intended to outline sides, so it's definitely nonsense, just on that alone. We are all siblings. There is no difference. But it becomes obvious when you consider that such behavior is contrary to our social inclination, anyway, as a species, and survival by extension. Just this simple recognition opens the door to envisioning alternatives grounded in human dignity and social justice.

By drawing on historical examples of communities and societies that successfully organized around principles of mutual aid and collective well-being, modern possibilities emerge that foster resilience and equity. For instance, recent initiatives and movements aiming to secure water as a fundamental public good—free from commodification and privatization—demonstrate that essential resources need not be controlled by market forces but can be managed democratically for the benefit of all (The Real News, 2019). Now imagine your life when all birthrights and human rights and needs within your experience are free, too. Furthermore, advances in technology and science hold tremendous potential to alleviate, rather than entrench, inequality and hardship. Now, imagine what life will be like when progress in science is made unabashedly, absent money, and/or politics getting in the way. When research and innovation are guided by public health, environmental sustainability, and equity goals, they can help dismantle systemic barriers that prevent equal access to life-saving treatments, clean energy, and sustainable infrastructure (Gallagher, 2017; Yeston et al., 2006). Now, imagine a life where trustworthy knowledge is just that, absent the influence of whatever gets paid for, or can be made popular.

Burl Minnis

WORLD PEACE

If you have any question about how this or that will actually happen after money; that's as simple as, "how do we do it now". Except, that your receipts will read 0.00. And, of course, we are all volunteers. But the way you treat your employees is very different than how you treat volunteers, so that's another benefit. You can beat your employees. Worldwide, today. We even wrote laws to say how you can't beat your employees. But everything else is fair game until we do figure it out. Try that with your volunteers and they won't be back. So, as the only organism ever in evolutionary biology that must work to survive, this may be the first time in 13,000 years that Man actually enjoys working, and becomes generalists again as a result.

Perhaps that is something that will look different, almost immediately; TV commercials. Instead of selling us stuff, corporations will be advertising that they still make stuff, and shifts are available, and all that. Or maybe in manufacturing; plastics would go away. We can blow mold bamboo pulp with the some of the same performance capabilities as the plastics they replace; bamboo pulp just chews up the molds too fast. Well, that sounds like a money problem and there ain't no more of that, so make more molds, or whatever. Or, if you want a house; all you need is the deed, and you get that right from the realtor. Just stop into an office and ask. When you're done with your house, just drop off your deed with any realtor. But, guaranteed there will be many other aspects of human experiences that become streamlined through reason and rational thinking.

It will be our generation that will have this the toughest, but that is only because we remember. But it's not just us as living entities. Corporations will also have to start doing things right. Online services, for instance, will have to be redesigned to service consumers without currency

WORLD PEACE

transactions, and that will have to be done on day one. The more things change, the more they stay the same; corporations undertake such titanic tasks daily, today, but all the effort goes into tasks securing our personal data. Interesting how all that goes away with money, too. And, since corporations will already be regearing and refitting to support volunteerism, and advertising shift availability, 35 days from the drop of this book will be plenty of time to hit the ground running as it were when world peace is enacted.

Central to these transformative efforts is the deliberate prioritization of human needs over profit maximization, a commitment to solidarity and cooperation rather than the perpetuation of artificially manufactured scarcity, and the democratization and decentralization of power in place of its concentration within elites and institutions (Aeon, 2017b; The Real News, 2018). The social, political, and economic structures that produce and maintain what we call "hardship" are rarely fundamental or immutable; they are human constructs, designed and maintained through choice and policy. As with any constructed system, they can be dismantled, restructured, and replaced by frameworks that promote true freedom. This realization offers both a critical hope and a mandate: to intentionally build societies that reflect our best values and capacities, rather than passively accept inherited limitations on human capabilities, potentials, and virtues.

Chapter 6: Truth, Reality, and Responsibility

Now it's Up to You

Throughout history, humanity has repeatedly stood at pivotal crossroads—moments when the choice lay between continuing down a well-worn, familiar path or summoning the collective courage to step into the unknown, challenging prevailing assumptions and forging new directions. Today, we find ourselves at just such a crucial juncture. The imperative before us is not only to acknowledge what is accurate about our shared condition but to translate that knowledge into purposeful action. While the information age promised a democratization of knowledge unprecedented in human history, it has paradoxically inundated us with overwhelming amounts of data, often leaving us uncertain of meaning, context, or responsibility. The lesson is clear: mere knowledge is insufficient unless coupled with personal and collective responsibility—we each bear an inescapable duty to engage and act (International Criminal Court [ICC], n.d.; OTP.InformationDesk@icc-cpi.int).

To distill this complex dynamic, consider the simple yet profound framework of the party game "Mafia," in which players are divided into two groups—those with hidden knowledge ("mafia") and the uninformed townspeople struggling to discern truth from deception (Wikipedia, n.d.-a). The town's survival depends on a collective commitment to rigorous inquiry and deliberation. If the responsibility for discerning truth is surrendered blindly to the loudest voices, the most powerful actors, or the most persuasive manipulators, disaster is inevitable. This game serves as a powerful microcosm of the moral predicament facing modern society. When distorted truths and misinformation are accepted uncritically, or when individuals abdicate their moral responsibility in favor of unquestioning obedience—a phenomenon known as the "agentic state"—people become mere instruments of authority, failing to acknowledge the consequences of their actions (American Psychological Association [APA], n.d.). Empirical research on the agentic state reveals how individuals subsumed within institutions or hierarchical structures often feel released from personal moral judgment, enabling participation in egregious crimes ranging from totalitarian atrocities to the banality of bureaucratic cruelty (APA, n.d.; ICC, n.d.).

Yet, history is not a deterministic machine powered solely by structural forces. This is our planet. Extensive archives, personal testimonies, and historical records confirm that individuals and communities, by refusing to passively accept inherited narratives and official versions of events, have repeatedly altered the course of history (Adams, 2021; International Criminal Court, n.d.). The establishment of international criminal justice mechanisms, such as the ICC, emerged from the determined refusal of peoples worldwide to tolerate impunity, demanding that even the most powerful individuals face consequences under ethical and legal standards (Rome Statute, 1998). While imperfect and contested, these advancements reflect a growing global consensus that each person shares in the stewardship of truth and justice. So, the mechanisms are there. Might as well use them. The POICC is expecting it, in fact.

The power of truth, however, depends fundamentally on its union with responsibility. Modern societies have witnessed

WORLD PEACE

the dire outcomes when moral agency is deflected, and myth is weaponized in service of power. Throughout history, peoples and cultures have been oppressed, entire communities erased, and mass atrocities rationalized through stories—be they religious interpretations, nationalist narratives, or economic doctrines—that legitimize suffering and subjugation (MSN, 2023). For example, colonial anthropological reinterpretations of Hindu mythology, designed to dehumanize and control, mirror contemporary economic dogmas that justify poverty and environmental degradation as necessary or natural, perpetuating cycles of harm born from distortion and falsehood (MSN, 2023; Quora, n.d.).

Legal doctrines such as sovereign immunity—intended to protect nations from external interference—have often shielded perpetrators of injustice from accountability, cloaking human rights violations behind the veil of national sovereignty (Wikipedia, n.d.-b; Wikipedia, n.d.-c). Nonetheless, waves of justice movements, from the post-World War II Nuremberg trials to South Africa's Truth and Reconciliation Commission, affirm that meaningful ethical progress arises when ordinary people refuse the passive inheritance of injustice and actively intervene (Jolly, 2018). The very foundation of social order and democratic governance pivots on the ability of individuals to transcend the "agentic state," reclaim moral agency, and engage in responsible, ethical action.

We inhabit an era of unparalleled documentation, record-keeping, and surveillance. The digital revolution has unleashed unprecedented ability to gather, store, and disseminate information globally (BBC, 2018). Yet, this wealth of data does not automatically translate to meaning, justice, or progress. When the curation, interpretation, and dissemination of knowledge are concentrated in the hands of narrow elites—or when apathy or distraction dulls public engagement with their own histories—the hard lessons of the past are lost or distorted (Adams, 2021). Philosopher David Hume, whose empiricism provided conceptual foundations for modern science, reminds us that reality's meaning is contingent on persistent inquiry—interpretation is a dynamic process woven into an unfolding narrative shaped by countless active agents over time (Brading, 2015).

The urgency of this moment cannot be overstated. We confront converging global crises: the sixth mass extinction event of the Anthropocene documented by leading scientific authorities including the National Science Foundation (NSF), pervasive social inequalities, persistent conflicts, and accelerating ecological devastation (Jolly, 2018; BBC, 2018; MSN, 2023). The era of passive observation has ended; witness alone is insufficient. Inspired by the South African model of restorative justice, the ethical imperative now is active intervention aimed at relieving suffering—whether that of humans, animals, individuals, or entire ecosystems (Johannson-Stenman, 2018).

History is, indeed, replete with the many humans who have stepped up for worthwhile causes and stood up to vilification for their efforts. Your voice on this matter will end all human misery, though. So, this is not those. This solution goes to the root cause, the keystone, and alleviates the system of all human misery at its core. Make no mistake; this is your one chance, and the last effort required by anyone for anything related to human rights violations or crimes against humanity or war crimes, forever.

Thus, the grand human experiment encompassing democracy, science, and law awaits its next era: one in which responsibility for truth and justice is no longer delegated to elites and bureaucracies alone but embraced collectively by all inhabitants of this fragile planet. As enshrined in the Rome Statute (1998), the essence of international justice is not retributive punishment but the affirmation of shared humanity and the mutual responsibilities it entails.

The Nature of Reality

For millennia, philosophers, scientists, and ordinary people alike have wrestled with profound questions about the nature of reality. Is reality an absolute, fixed, and objective condition that exists independent of human perception, or is it a fluid, dynamic construct shaped continuously by context, consensus, and contestation of human imagination? Physical reality is as constant as "I think therefore I am". Human perception of qualified reality, then, is always a product of the five senses. More so necessary, today, than in the time of Descartes, however.

Centuries of reflective inquiry suggest that reality is far from static; rather, it is constantly being negotiated and redefined by social interactions, power relations, and collective beliefs. As Solman (2017) articulates, reality emerges as a contingent phenomenon, constantly evolving through the values we choose to prioritize, the investments we make, and the legacies we seek to preserve. Bostrom's insights, as cited by Solman, highlight this complexity by emphasizing how our shared reality is, in essence, the sum of collective human choices about what matters most. Now, reality is not just what we know as real, but what we imagine as real, as well.

Compelling research now challenges the assumption that even our most fundamental categories—whether in medicine, economics, identity, or ethics—are natural or immutable. For instance, diagnoses of mental illness often defy clear biological boundaries; symptoms frequently overlap and blur diagnostic categories, revealing that these labels are as much products of social negotiation, cultural context, and historical circumstance as of biological realities (Aeon, 2018a).

Ideology is a conative toxin, and greed a mental malady catalyst exacerbating other human frailties. The same fluidity applies to economic systems and cultural identities, which are shaped profoundly by history, power, and human agency. The global dominance of the U.S. dollar in the oil trade, for example, is not governed by any natural law but is the outcome of a complex interplay of political decisions, military interventions, and economic strategizing that has unfolded over decades (Quora, n.d.). Oil is energy. Humans need energy to persist. Oil is a fact. Money is fiction. Change the value of the USD fiction in this case and our oil fact becomes unattainable. In this case, our ability to raise fire. And that's a birthright. Threatened because of a fiction. The nature of reality, today, therefore includes more than the physical and/or tangible because fiction failures are just as impactful.

Travel experiences in culturally rich environments such as Fiji provide vivid examples of how reality is mediated through tradition, communal memory, and evolving norms. Access to villages in Fiji is rigorously regulated, reflecting

Burl Minnis

WORLD PEACE

generations of negotiated understandings about belonging, hospitality, and shared responsibility (BBC, 2017a). These practices are not arbitrary restrictions but embody a deeply rooted social contract that balances respect for collective heritage with present-day realities. Because these represent sociocultural ethnocentrisms, they are given the respect of reality, often codified into law.

Similarly, persistent gender pay-gaps worldwide illustrate the tension between evolving social ideals and enduring structural inequalities. Despite broad cultural commitments to gender equality, women, on average, continue to earn less than men—a disparity perpetuated not simply by overt discrimination but by the complex weaving of habit, tradition, and vested interests that maintain social "reality" beyond mere factual truth (PBS, 2017a). Just get rid of money and no pay-gaps exist. No gender inequality, nor comparison and/or contrast between genders whatsoever, and certainly no quota systems.

The rapid rise of modern technologies only deepens the complexity of constructing and understanding reality today. Platforms of social media, television networks, and news cycles selectively amplify certain voices while marginalizing others, often privileging scandal, sensationalism, and polarizing content over measured accuracy and nuance (BBC, 2018; Thomas, 2017). The international spread and standardization of television formats demonstrate how cultural understandings of "reality" can be commodified, replicated, and exported on a global scale, shaping collective perception in profound ways (Thomas, 2017). Meanwhile, digital privacy violations, massive data breaches, and ongoing surveillance practices

WORLD PEACE

have become so normalized that their ethical ramifications rarely provoke sustained public outcry or reflection, despite their extraordinary implications for autonomy and justice (CNN, 2019).

Yet, as monolithic and synchronized as consensus may sometimes seem, reality remains fundamentally contested terrain. The so-called "information arms race," characterized by battles over narratives and truth, is perhaps unwinnable in absolute terms, but the necessity of persistent engagement is non-negotiable (Rose, 2020). Philosopher Hannah Arendt's concept of the banality of evil underscores that moral failures often arise not from malevolence but from thoughtlessness—a readiness to accept degraded, simplified versions of reality that serve prevailing power structures. Such complacency leads consensus to become complicity in injustice. Recognition of the hidden power dynamics behind accepted "truths" insists that vigilance is not optional but foundational to any liberation project (Brading, 2015; Rose, 2020). Well, here's a fundamental reality to hold onto: as a species, we're already extinct. Nothing will ever save us. If our lives were defined by the dash between the two dates on our tombstone, what will your dash say about you? Science—heroic in its commitments to objectivity and empirical rigor—is itself subject to continual revision and reinterpretation. Revolutionary proposals, such as the experimental freezing of critically ill patients, challenge long-held definitions of life and death, showing how these core concepts resist simple, fixed delineation (Aeon, 2018b). Likewise, evolutionary theory is evolving. New findings reveal that behaviors traditionally considered peripheral, such as grandmotherly care and multi-generational social bonds, significantly shape human survival, adding richness and complexity to models that once narrowly emphasized reproductive fitness alone (Aeon, 2018c).

Cultural theorists warn against uncritical adherence to a "human-centered" worldview, illuminating how privileging humanity above all else can sanction exploitation and justify neglect across species boundaries. This anthropocentric hubris risks fostering shallow and unstable ideals of dignity and justice (Johannson-Stenman, 2018; Sussman, 2019). The intertwined crises of climate change, biodiversity loss, and zoonotic pandemics demonstrate the inescapable interconnectedness of all life, dissolving comforting binaries that historically justified human exceptionalism and selfishness.

Even collective memories of social unrest or riot—often depicted in official histories as chaos or criminality— emerge, under deeper analysis, as vital engines of democratic creativity, renewal, and resistance (Street, 2018). These challenges to dominant mythologies are not merely oppositional acts but essential correctives that ensure the evolving "reality" remains open and responsive to voices historically excluded from power: the poor, marginalized, dissenters, and oppressed (Street, 2018).

The moral imperative, therefore, is unmistakable: reality, like history, is not a fixed tableau but an ongoing process of construction, contestation, and potential improvement. To renounce responsibility for shaping reality is not an act of philosophical humility but an abdication of historical and ethical duty. While it all may seem so insurmountable, and highly convoluted, and next to impossible to negotiate the multitude of imagined realities simultaneously; try abolishing money and see how clear, simple, and basic reality becomes then.

Truth and Accuracy

The survival and flourishing of any society fundamentally depend on the collective capacity to discern reality from illusion, to distinguish what is genuinely fact from what is merely expedient or convenient stories about those facts. In the 21st century, however, this fundamental epistemic task faces profound challenges. We live amidst an epistemological crisis characterized by a widespread cultural and political skepticism toward truth itself—a pervasive sense that truth is negotiable, that expert knowledge is discretionary rather than authoritative, and that accuracy holds less sway than compelling persuasion (Lutz, 1989; Politifact, 2016; BBC, 2017b). This destabilization of truth threatens the very foundations upon which social trust and democratic governance rest. Once truth becomes decoupled from fact, two different realities occur. One predicated on factual reality, the other on an imagined story about those facts. Thus, undermining the value of truth as being relegated to source-dependent opinion.

Philosophers have long debated the nature of truth, and their inquiries form a deep and complex tradition. Various theories offer differing perspectives: the correspondence theory posits that a statement is true if it accurately reflects objective reality or facts in the world; the coherence theory suggests truth is constituted by the harmonization and logical consistency of a set of beliefs within a system; pragmatist accounts emphasize that truth is what proves useful or "works" effectively within lived experience (Brading, 2015). Regardless of the theoretical lens employed, however, truth loses its transformative power when decoupled from essential intellectual virtues such as humility, curiosity, and open dialogue. Without these, truth becomes rigid, dogmatic, or weaponized.

For the purpose of this work, truth and accuracy are treated as contemporary experiences, globally. And, they are not the same things. In all human events, in anything that might transpire in our experience, there is the cold, hard, calculable, quantifiable facts of the matter. That which we call the accuracy. Then, there is everyone's individual story about those facts. That which we call the truth. In as much as you can never guarantee that any two, or more, people, will ever perceive the same event, in exactly the same way; truth, then, can be said to be purely source-dependent. And, no one's truth is any more, or less, valid than anyone else's; it's just the way the facts occurred to them.

Truth, therefore, is not absolute. But accuracy always is, as facts always are. For instance, you may ask as many people as you want, who witnessed an accident; "what happened", and you will get as many different answers back, as people you've asked. And, no one's answer will be any more, or less, valid than anyone else's; it is just the way the facts of the matter occurred to them. And, that individual perception of reality, that source dependent truth, is what we permit to be called the truth, today. There will always be certain facts that punctuate the story of what happened, like in an automotive accident, for example. Like, it was a bus, not a motorcycle. Or, it happened during the day, rather than at night. Or, it happened in the middle of the block, rather than the corner. There are certain facts. Imagine a bus goes through an intersection, for instance, and hits three

WORLD PEACE

pedestrians. A bystander on the curb might say something to the effect that; "he didn't even try to stop, he just barreled through the intersection, and plowed all those people over".

Well, that could be a fair assessment of what was perceived as happening, but hardly the facts of what accurately happened. In fact, the bus driver might not have been a "he" at all. Perhaps, "he" was a "she", in fact. But the bystander wouldn't have been able to see that from the curb. So, the bystander's story of that fact was that the bus driver was a he, and, as such, that is the bystander's truth about the matter. And, it might not have been that the bus driver didn't care to stop, as the bystander insisted, the bus driver might, simply, have had a heart attack in the middle of the block, and had already been dead by the time the bus got to the intersection. The bystander wouldn't have realized that from the curb, either. So, the truth to the bystander is that the incident was intentional.

But that's just one pedestrian example (no pun intended) of a much more comprehensive occurrence in human experience. Truth is always a fictional construct of the perceiver, predicated on the perception of facts, but rarely anywhere near accurate, today. Hold up your hand, for example, and ask someone what he, and/or she, sees. Someone may reply; "five fingers", while someone else might reply; "four fingers, and a thumb", and still someone else specifying a right, or left, hand, depending on which one you hold up. Truth is how those facts occurred to them, and none of them was, actually, wrong. But, nonetheless, none of them were factual, either, nor entirely accurate. It's why Rorschach tests work. It's what the politics ideology counts on buffooning wedge issues, for instance. It's how swindles are made.

As such, the label of "truth" about anything can serve as a powerful tool for the manipulation of reality when perpetuating a swindle. It is how truth became detached from accuracy all those thousands of years in this Age of the Swindle.

Modern communication technologies have simultaneously expanded access to facts while complicating its pursuit. Podcasts, documentaries, and digital platforms have democratized the dissemination of information, enabling diverse perspectives and deeper understanding. Yet these same technologies also facilitate the formation of echo chambers, filter bubbles, and the proliferation of doublespeak—a linguistic strategy deliberately designed to obfuscate, manipulate, and control rather than clarify and enlighten (Galer, 2017; Lutz, 1989). The global spread of "alternative facts," conspiracy theories, and systematic propaganda illustrates the nuanced ways in which truth can be distorted and weaponized on unprecedented scales (BBC, 2018; CNN, 2017).

The consequences of such distortions are not abstract or hypothetical; they inflict real suffering across populations. History teaches us that expert testimony is often dismissed when it conflicts with prevailing ideologies, inconvenient data is suppressed, and rigorous investigation is subordinated to political agendas (BBC, 2018; Lutz, 1989). Propaganda campaigns meticulously construct narratives that demonize and dehumanize targeted groups, laying the groundwork for mass atrocities and social divisions (Rose, 2020). In today's age of "deniability," the manipulation and denial of truth constitute powerful instruments in perpetuating injustice.

Doublespeak by William D. Lutz, highlights how language can be carefully engineered to disguise brutal realities— using euphemisms like "revenue enhancement" for tax increases, "terminal living" for euthanasia, or "collateral damage" for civilian casualties in war (Lutz, 1989; Wikipedia, n.d.-d). Stripped of precision and ethical grounding, such language transforms truth from a source of empowerment into a tool of confusion and poison.

In response, the rise of journalistic "fact-checking" initiatives illustrates both the urgent need for verifiable truth and the profound difficulty of ascertaining it in an environment awash with information and competing influences (Politifact, 2016). Critics refer to this challenge as the "triage of truth," emphasizing that discerning fact from falsehood requires active, critical engagement by the public rather than passive acceptance of purported expertise (Rose, 2020).

This challenge is further complicated by the often invisible but significant costs associated with technological and scientific "progress." For example, the environmental toll of consumer electronics—ranging from resource extraction to hazardous e-waste—remains largely hidden from public view but poses critical threats to planetary health and sustainability (IEEE, 2004). In domains spanning environmental science, medicine, sports, and public health, the stakes attached to truthfulness and accuracy transcend academic debate; they become matters of survival itself.

Institutions entrusted with education and media production bear a frontline responsibility in this ongoing battle for epistemic integrity. Educational curricula that confront historically uncomfortable truths—about Thanksgiving, Columbus's legacy, and the foundational myths underpinning societies—represent essential efforts not only to transmit knowledge but to nurture ethical habits of critical inquiry, empathy, and informed skepticism among future generations (PBS, 2017b; Street, 2018).

No one needs to die for world peace; that's true. But nothing needs to be destroyed, nor erased from history, either. Unlike every other massively destructive event to transpire throughout human history, whenever theology, or ideology, came to town, world peace embraces the past as a clear indicator of our departure from, and return to, rational human reason. And. humans are nothing without history.

Ultimately, our contemporary "epistemic crisis" is inseparable from ethical concerns (Rose, 2020). A society that shrugs off lies validates apathy and ideology, creating fertile ground for violence and division. Only a cultural and institutional ethos committed to continuous correction—marked by the humility to admit mistakes, the courage to challenge prevailing consensus, and the resilience to engage in ongoing dialogue—can foster a world in which truth-seeking is foundational, trusted, and just once again.

The Responsibility of Change

To possess knowledge is not to be absolved of accountability. Deep understanding of the forces that construct and define reality—along with the mechanisms of distortion and the philosophical foundations of truth—

WORLD PEACE

imposes upon each individual a profound moral and practical obligation to act. History demonstrates with painful clarity that mass atrocities, systemic oppression, and ecological devastation do not arise solely from the malevolence of a few bad actors, but are perpetuated equally through the widespread indifference, inertia, and passive compliance of many (International Criminal Court [ICC], n.d.; OTP.InformationDesk@icc-cpi.int). This collective abdication of responsibility allows destructive systems to persist and expand unchecked.

You never obligate a human being. It can get you killed, as it is tantamount to involuntary servitude, if not simply bad manners. Humans obligate themselves. You don't. for instance, tell anyone, "You owe me for this…" They will tell you that. So, I can't obligate you to this contribution. You must commit to doing this yourself. Do it, or don't do it. But make that decision because it's what you want to do. Then, contribute your voice as a rational reasonable member of the human majority. The POICC is expecting your correspondence.

If human civilization is to endure beyond mere persistence—and if principles such as justice, dignity, and sustainability are to transcend empty rhetoric and become living realities—then responsibility cannot remain the exclusive province of institutions or elites. Rather, it must be embraced by each person, in every community and nation. We must critically examine the stories we tell ourselves and others: What narratives shape our worldview? Which truths do we actively defend with courage and integrity? What constructed "realities" do we accept passively, and what are their true costs—socially, environmentally, and ethically?

WORLD PEACE

The major systems that scaffold our lives—economic structures, legal frameworks, cultural traditions, and media ecosystems—are not fixed or immutable entities. They are human creations, perpetually subject to influence, reform, or rupture through engaged and informed participation.

The urgency of the moment in history is profound and unambiguous. As enshrined in the Rome Statute (1998) and underscored by the ongoing work of the ICC, even the gravest global crimes—genocide, crimes against humanity, and war crimes—are now subject to the scrutiny and accountability mechanisms that ordinary citizens may evoke and support since ratification in 2002. Philosophers, scientists, writers, and activists over generations have made it clear that responsibility is not merely a theoretical ideal; it is non-negotiable and intrinsic to the condition of freedom itself. To claim liberty without the willingness to bear responsibility is to invoke a hollow freedom that ultimately facilitates tyranny and harm. The majority of humans do not do the politics ideology. You can see Figure 2 for evidence of that, in the USD, at least. But everyone must do the monetary economy ideology. And, it is as simple to turn off as, setting all general ledgers to zero. Even corporations record a net-net of zero in the black, so everyone and everything remains happy and unchanged in their processes.

The call is, unequivocally, up to you. The pathway to transformative change is rarely comfortable, and never neatly marked, but it remains an essential journey. As Voltaire astutely warned, "Those who can make you believe absurdities can make you commit atrocities." The margin between apathy and advocacy, between complicity and courage, is measured through our individual and collective

WORLD PEACE

acts of responsibility. Every conscious choice to discern truth, to speak out, and to act justly chips away at the structures of oppression, moving us closer to a world where freedom, peace, and humanity prevail. But I cannot obligate you. It's a responsibility you must recognize and adopt. The, do it, or don't do it, but make that decision because it is what you want to do. And, no one needs to die for world peace. We are all in this together.

Part III
Human Rights Violation

Chapter 7: Law and the Institutionalization of Fiction
Law: When the Tool Becomes the Cage

In principle, the law stands as one of society's most fundamental pillars of rationality and order—a structured system designed to transform the inherently messy, complex realities of human experience into clear, codified rules, defined rights, and equitable remedies. Reason is the soul of law, as they say. It promises a framework through which disputes can be fairly adjudicated, social contracts enforced, and justice administered. Yet, in practice, the law functions far more ambiguously and is frequently wielded as an instrument of power by those who shape and control it. Regardless of how objectively crafted or democratically ratified it may be, law inevitably encodes a set of fictions, assumptions, and priority judgments. 99% of all laws on the books, for instance, govern ownership. These embedded fictions determine what society values, delineate who enjoys protection and privileges and who remains vulnerable and marginalized, and define what phenomena are recognized as real or conveniently ignored (Bastiat, 1850/2013; Foundation for Economic Education [FEE], 2015; Wikipedia, n.d.-a).

The French economist and philosopher Frédéric Bastiat poignantly captures this enduring tension when he writes, "When law and morality contradict each other, the citizen has the cruel alternative of either losing his moral sense or losing his respect for the law" (Bastiat, 1850/2013, p. 50). This dilemma remains strikingly relevant centuries later. The law often compels the public and institutions alike to treat legal fictions—conceptual constructs that exist solely within the legal framework—as if they were objective truths external to human invention. A pregnant woman, for instance, is killed. It's two homicides. A woman has an abortion and homicide isn't even a consideration. So, invariably, every citizen of that jurisdiction permits and condones murder. Such fictions, also, include doctrines and principles like "corporate personhood," which confers on corporations' certain rights and responsibilities akin to those of individuals; "sovereign immunity," which shields states and governmental actors from certain forms of legal accountability; and "malum prohibitum," a category of offenses defined not by inherent immorality but by legislative fiat (Wikiquote, n.d.; Wikipedia, n.d.-b; Wikipedia, n.d.-c; Wikipedia, n.d.-d).

While these legal constructs serve administrative and regulatory functions, they often disproportionately benefit powerful institutions, entrench inequality, and obscure the lived realities of individuals. They transform abstract legal instruments into cages that constrain justice, accountability, and social progress, frequently subordinating substantive ethics to procedural formalism. Consequently, law becomes less a servant of the people and more a self-perpetuating mechanism that reinforces existing hierarchies and privileges under the guise of neutrality and universality.

Constructed Legality: Fictions That Disrupt Reality

The law has historically operated through the construction and maintenance of fictions—legal constructs that stand apart from lived, physical reality but wield extraordinary influence over social, economic, and political life. One foundational example is the Roman concept of "legal persons," which designates entities—such as corporations or organizations—as holders of rights and responsibilities, independent of individual human beings. This abstraction allowed monarchs in medieval Europe and later modern corporate titans to cloak their interests behind legal shields, protecting assets while diffusing personal accountability and responsibility (Wikipedia, n.d.-a). The evolving legal personality of corporations now facilitates complex structures of ownership and liability that often insulate powerful actors from direct consequences of their actions.

Comparable legal fictions permeate modern institutions that profoundly affect daily life. Health insurance, for instance, began as an unusual and debated historical model in many parts of the world but has now become deeply enmeshed within legal frameworks, economic imperatives, and social policies. Over time, the original intents—to provide care, mitigate risk, and serve populations—have often been obscured or compromised, eclipsed by bureaucratic complexity and profit-driven motives (Wikipedia, n.d.-e). The prevailing fiction that regards health as a "commodity" commodifies well-being itself, institutionalizing gatekeeping, rationing of access, and exclusion of vulnerable populations (Aljazeera, 2017).

Similarly, the "rule of law" is widely venerated as a hallmark of just governance, purportedly serving as a bulwark against arbitrariness and tyranny. However, in practice, the rules themselves are malleable and are routinely rewritten or selectively enforced to entrench the power of dominant interests and preserve existing hierarchies (Sng & Moriguchi, 2014; BBC, 2018a; Storrs, 2018). The British Empire's asserted commitment to the rule of law stood in stark contrast to its simultaneous role in systems of racialized exclusion, colonial expropriation, and economic exploitation, exposing the contradictions inherent in legal claims to universality and fairness (Dorsett, 2017). Within the United States, the legal distinction between "malum in se" (wrong in itself) and "malum prohibitum" (wrong because legally prohibited) further illustrates how much of legality depends not on inherent morality but on social context and political determinations. Laws under the category of malum prohibitum are often arbitrary and subject to change, highlighting the contingency and constructed nature of legal norms (Wikipedia, n.d.-c).

Contemporary legal regimes extend these abstractions into previously unimagined domains. Instruments that appear neutral or technical—such as copyright laws, data privacy regulations, anti-jaywalking ordinances, and digital copyright enforcement mechanisms—have increasingly become vehicles for cementing commercial monopolies, enhancing surveillance capacities, and enabling intrusive state and corporate oversight (BBC, 2018b; BBC, 2018c; Wikipedia, n.d.-f). Complex legal language and institutional practices cloak these policies, justifying them with appeals to procedural correctness, intellectual property rights, or public order. In reality, many of these laws prioritize institutional convenience and economic interests over the public good, constructing elaborate fictions that serve to suppress dissent, restrict freedoms, and rationalize systemic inequalities (Electronic Frontier Foundation [EFF], n.d.; Indystar, 2018).

The Sublimation of Justice into Procedure

The power of law resides not only in the substantive outcomes it prescribes but also—perhaps more insidiously—in the ways it is justified, rationalized, and ritualized, especially when its applications veer into manifest injustice. This is why you never codify society. Society changes as it wants. Codification changes are glacially slow under tort reform. Legal reasoning often cloaks itself in traditions and precedents that reach deep into history, invoking venerable concepts of governance and statecraft. For example, legal debates about privacy frequently appeal to long-standing principles once grounded in the physical and geographical limits of sovereign authority. Yet, in the digital age, these traditions have evolved—or arguably devolved—into sprawling empires of data extraction and surveillance, with courts serving as the final bastions defending these interests (BBC, 2017a). The adoption of legal fictions in this context is far from arbitrary. They constitute deliberate mechanisms through which powerful systems maintain their durability and legitimacy, masking the concentration of benefits in the hands of a select few behind opaque veneers of "due process," "objectivity," or the amorphous abstraction of "national interest" (Foundation for Economic Education [FEE], 2015; Aeon, 2018a; National Public Radio [NPR], 2019). Computers, for instance, required just such mechanisms in order to seem relevant and make a buck. Today, you cannot have identity theft without computers, you cannot have piracy without computers, you can't have untrustworthy knowledge, you can't even have those same computers, today, without producing four times more power than we're producing today, globally. Just so some A.I. company can make a buck. Now, imagine what laws will govern A.I. when we anthropomorphize everything to pursue and acquire money at all costs, by Charters.

This overvaluation of legal form at the expense of ethical substance finds illustrative expression in the pervasive use of mandatory arbitration clauses embedded in contracts across employment, consumer goods, and financial services sectors. Such clauses compel workers, consumers, and vulnerable parties to forgo their constitutionally guaranteed rights to a public and impartial trial, instead consigning disputes to private tribunals that overwhelmingly favor industry interests (Reclaim Democracy, n.d.-a). The institutionalization of arbitration as a dominant dispute resolution mechanism exemplifies a broader trend wherein legal institutions prioritize efficiency, predictability, and commercial interests over fairness and genuine accountability.

Moreover, this retreat from substantive justice is reflected in judicial rulings that systematically erode worker protections, restrict access to class action lawsuits, and weaken consumer protection laws. The United States Supreme Court, for example, has delivered a series of decisions diminishing collective legal recourse, effectively narrowing the capacity for redress against systemic abuses (The Real News Network [TRNN], 2018a). Such decisions cloak themselves in the rhetoric of "legal certainty," "stability," and respect for contractual freedom, yet they risk alienating individuals from meaningful participation in justice and leave systemic wrongs unaddressed.

The nice thing is that when money goes away, we will all become volunteers. And the way you treat your volunteers is very different than the way you treat employees. We can beat our employees, today, worldwide. We even have laws that say how we cannot. But everything else in human experience as a laborer is still fair game until we figure out it's a beating. Matters of volunteer relations and retention will become the only important labor rights that nonliving entities will need to consider.

In sum, modern law functions as a sophisticated masterclass in the institutionalization of fiction. It pretends that abstract legal formulas can neatly parse notions of compensation, liability, or personal identity as though these were mere calculable variables. It equates the complex, lived realities of human beings with the privileges and protections afforded to legal abstractions—corporations, trusts, or sovereign entities—thereby distancing law from its foundational purpose: to serve justice for living, breathing individuals and communities.

Forcing Nonsense to Make Sense

When the law distorts reality, its most insidious function is its capacity to transform nonsense into what society comes to accept as common sense. Have you ever read a Terms of Service Agreement, for instance? Through the use of densely layered legal language, intricate and often circular reasoning, and relentless institutional repetition, complex or even absurd concepts are normalized and ingrained as immutable truths. These constructed "realities" function much like the fable of "The Emperor's New Clothes," except amplified and imposed upon billions of people worldwide, who are socialized to participate in and reinforce these illusions without question (Aeon, 2018b). This process effectively masks contradictions, obscures power imbalances, and suppresses critical inquiry, causing individuals to internalize and perpetuate systemic absurdities as natural and inevitable facets of the social order.

Normalizing Absurdities

Economist Joseph Stiglitz astutely observed that law often operates without interrogating the fundamental question: "In whose interest?" (Stiglitz, 2002). This oversight facilitates the naturalization and perpetuation of economic dogmas that, while culturally ingrained, fail critical scrutiny.

WORLD PEACE

Foremost among these is the dominant belief that employment—specifically, paid jobs—is the singular source of human dignity, social value, and identity. This conviction has been so deeply embedded into legal frameworks, social policies, and fiscal governance that questioning it has become nearly taboo, even as mounting challenges such as rapid automation, escalating mental health crises, and ecological breakdown fundamentally undermine the premise that jobs, as currently conceived, sustain society's well-being (Graeber, 2018; Aeon, 2016a).

This ideological entrenchment is evident in the widespread imposition of compulsory work paradigms. Welfare-to-work initiatives, stringent conditions attached to unemployment benefits, and the systemic marginalization of caregiving and creative labor all rely on legal fictions that assert "work" as an inherent moral good and universal obligation. This belief obscures the reality that such labor regimes often serve as contingent, historically situated responses to socio-economic challenges that may no longer exist—or have evolved beyond those frameworks (Aeon, 2016a). These policies persist, not because they represent rational or humane solutions, but because they are structurally codified within legal, economic, and bureaucratic systems, defended through procedural rationales that insulate them from scrutiny of their profound human costs (Robinson, 2009).

Parallel dysfunctions manifest across regulatory and legal domains. Patent laws, for example, originally designed to incentivize innovation, increasingly function as mechanisms to stifle competition, consolidate corporate monopolies, and restrict creative progress (The Real News Network [TRNN], 2018b). Municipal efforts to ban homelessness from public spaces—under the guise of "quality of life" ordinances—criminalize poverty and obscure structural causes beneath superficial legal rationales. More subtly, law enacts racialized exclusions through everyday mechanisms such as dress codes, credit checks, the collection and use of biometric data, and policing practices like "stop and frisk" that disproportionately target marginalized communities (New York Times, 2006; BBC, 2017b; Aeon, 2017a; CNN, 2017a). These legal and regulatory tools collectively maintain systemic inequalities under the guise of neutrality and standardization.

At its core, the law compels individuals and communities to act as if constructed legal realities are true and just, even when their lived experiences reveal profound contradictions and injustices. The concept of malum prohibitum—offenses that are wrong solely because they are prohibited by law, rather than inherently immoral—perfectly encapsulates this dynamic. Such rules exist not because they are grounded in ethical truth, but because the legal system has arbitrarily declared them necessary, often to maintain order or authority (Wikipedia, n.d.-c). This phenomenon reflects what some scholars describe as the "iron cage" of modernity: not a cage forged of physical steel, but one wrought from the constraints of mind, custom, and the normalization of legalistic rationality over substantive justice.

The Weaponization of Legitimacy

In contemporary society, where legal frameworks often sanctify the accumulation of profit while simultaneously penalizing human need, what commands public respect and obedience is less the intrinsic justice or efficacy of legal outcomes than the legitimacy ascribed to the procedural appearance of those outcomes. This phenomenon—the weaponization of legitimacy—transforms law from a principled guide toward equity into a tool used to entrench existing power structures and marginalize dissenting voices. For example, the architectural complexity of national and international tax systems enables billionaires and multinational corporations to exploit loopholes and pay little to no taxes, while ordinary working-class citizens bear a disproportionate tax burden. This disparity is starkly revealed in investigations such as the Panama Papers of 2016 or the Paradise Papers of 2017 or the Pandora Papers of 2021, and the work of the International Consortium of Investigative Journalists (ICIJ), which expose how wealth is protected and legalized through intricate financial engineering, while social safety nets and public services are starved of resources (BBC, 2017c; Paradise Papers, BBC News, 2017; ICIJ, 2018).

Concomitantly, the legal right—and democratic imperative—of individuals and groups to challenge authority has increasingly come under assault through the deployment of restrictive laws and regulations. Whether through protest, whistleblowing, or critical journalism, social movements striving for systemic transformation face escalating barriers. These include expansive surveillance practices, anti-protest ordinances, and laws criminalizing dissent—all of which serve to fence out radical change and preserve the prevailing order under the guise of maintaining "system stability" (Electronic Frontier Foundation [EFF], n.d.; Dorsett, 2017). The legal system thus functions as a gatekeeper, safeguarding entrenched interests by systematically circumscribing the scope and efficacy of opposition.

Such dynamics are undergirded by a repertoire of legitimizing myths and fictions routinely invoked in legal and political theory. Concepts such as "natural law," "sovereign will," and the sanctity of social contracts or majority rule are repeatedly deployed as rhetorical and doctrinal justifications for enforcing compliance. These abstractions serve as ideological cover, camouflaging coercion behind the language of consent and moral order (The Real News Network [TRNN], 2018c; Aeon, 2018a; Mills, 2017). This is no mere procedural anomaly or accidental by-product but rather the essential logic of law as ideological apparatus: a system designed not just to regulate behavior but to manufacture consensus and ritualize submission to constructed fictions. Through this process, legitimacy becomes both weapon and shield—coercing conformity while masking power relations in the guise of impartial justice.

Shills for Ideology

One of the most insidious and dangerous functions of law is its role as a mouthpiece—or shill—for prevailing ideologies. Legal systems do not operate in isolation or neutral objectivity; rather, they are deeply embedded in and permeated by the dominant ideological frameworks that shape society's values and priorities. These ideologies determine which behaviors, groups, and interests are deemed worthy of protection, which acts are justified forms of punishment, and crucially, whose suffering is acknowledged, minimized, or dismissed.

Through this dynamic, the law takes on the role of codifying and legitimizing the prevailing worldview, transmitting and reinforcing ideological narratives across generations. It frames justice in terms consistent with the interests of dominant social, economic, and political classes, often at the expense of marginalized populations whose lived realities do not align with the ideological assumptions embedded in legal frameworks. Thus, law becomes a vehicle for systemic bias, perpetuating inequality and shaping societal norms according to ideological imperatives rather than universal principles of fairness or human dignity.

Legal Systems as Vectors of Repressive Ideology

Modern legal systems frequently claim a posture of neutrality and impartiality, presenting themselves as objective frameworks designed to administer justice and uphold societal order. However, these systems are deeply embedded with implicit and explicit assumptions that primarily reflect the interests, power dynamics, and worldviews of those who create, interpret, and enforce the laws (Wikipedia, n.d.-g; Britannica, n.d.). Under the rhetorical banners of "public order," "national security," or "market rationality," legal institutions have historically been co-opted and weaponized in the service of imperial expansion, maintenance of racial hierarchies, and the facilitation of economic extraction (Dorsett, 2017; Chomsky, 2003; Aeon, 2017b).

A concrete illustration of this dynamic can be found in the Cold War era, which gave rise to comprehensive architectures of "national emergency" law. These laws sanctioned pervasive surveillance, authorized indefinite detention without due process, and normalized extraordinary security "states of exception"—extra-legal practices justified by the purported necessity of national defense. During WWII, the US even invented an entirely new energy arm to be added to the list of bludgeoning, cutting edge, chemical, biological, and projectile arms already in the arsenal and already guaranteed to the citizens as a right. And the US did it in secret, without consent of the governed. Not even consultation. And all under the auspices of national security. Now, Americans have the right to bear all six different arms. These precedents have since been institutionalized and expanded in contemporary contexts, enabling mass data collection programs and curtailing civil liberties under the guise of combating modern threats (Aeon, 2018c; Centers for Disease Control and Prevention [CDC], 2020; Wake Forest University, 2020). Consequently, the legal apparatus has become a foundational tool for extending and perpetuating state power in ways that profoundly impact individual freedoms.

In the pharmaceutical and biotechnology sectors, so-called legal "innovation" further exemplifies this instrumentalization of law. Intellectual property regimes—particularly patents—have been privileged over accessibility, equity, and the public good. This translates into a system where patients are primarily treated as consumers constrained by market mechanisms, and researchers operate as legal subjects within a labyrinth of proprietary rights and competitive secrecy rather than collaborative public service (Science Daily, 2008; Robinson, 2009; Aeon, 2017c). The legal frameworks thus shape not only the economics of healthcare and technology but also the lived experiences and possibilities of health and science.

Legal education, which outwardly promotes critical analytical skills and the neutral transmission of jurisprudential knowledge, is in fact saturated with entrenched assumptions about which populations warrant protection, whose pain is legitimized, and whose interests are prioritized. From court cases addressing affirmative action policies in universities to the criminalization and stigmatization of migrants and refugees, legal reasoning is frequently manipulated and contorted to produce rulings that align with broader political agendas and power structures

(CNN, 2017b; Aeon, 2018a; NPR, 2019). Far from being a neutral arbiter, law often functions as a performative tool shaping social realities in accordance with hegemonic ideologies.

At its core, the law elevates process above substantive outcomes: it values procedure more than justice, compliance more than emancipation. Paradoxically, the law is often most meticulously technical precisely at the points where it is least just. As legal historian Imre Lakatos observed, "the law is not an end in itself, but a tool—whose purpose depends on who wields it, and whose dreams it makes real" (Lakatos, 1978; Aeon, 2018d). This insight underlines the inherently political and ideological character of legal systems and challenges the assumption that law is a neutral or universally benevolent mechanism.

News, 'Reality,' and Legal Ideology

The intricate relationship between media and law constitutes a symbiotic mirror of narratives, wherein each reinforces and shapes the other. In contemporary society, news cycles do more than merely report events; they actively participate in constructing and reproducing the fictions of the legal system. Complex realities—systems marked by layers of institutional power, legal intricacies, and socio-political dynamics—are often reduced to simplistic, polarized debates. These narratives obscure the deeper institutional frameworks that facilitate systemic abuses and inequalities, rendering the intricate mechanisms behind legal decisions largely invisible to public scrutiny (Baraniuk, 2018; Mihala, 2017; Asseraf, 2017; Aeon, 2017d).

The widespread concern over "fake news" and manipulation within social media platforms is not an incidental

WORLD PEACE

phenomenon but an integral aspect of a broader epistemic shift. Within this shift, law and public opinion are co-constructed processes that mutually reinforce constructed fictions to secure ideological advantage. The boundaries between truth, misinformation, and fiction blur as narratives are curated to serve particular political or economic interests, shaping public perceptions in ways that align with established power structures (BBC, 2017d; ProPublica, 2018).

Legal mechanisms ostensibly designed to combat misinformation—such as defamation laws, digital copyright enforcement filters, and regulatory attempts at controlling online speech—frequently serve dual roles. Rather than providing neutral, unbiased protections for truth and public safety, these tools are weaponized to suppress dissent, intimidate critics, and fortify the fragile boundaries of "acceptable" discourse. In practice, they act as gatekeeping instruments, reinforcing the hegemonic ideologies embedded within the legal and political systems rather than promoting genuine transparency or democratic participation (BBC, 2018b; BBC, 2018c; Southern California University [SCU], n.d.).

Consequently, society increasingly normalizes the institutionalization of fiction as a background condition—an almost invisible and uncontroversial feature of daily life. This normalization permeates various domains, from criminal "justice" systems that prioritize punitive measures over restorative approaches, to environmental regulations overwhelmingly shaped and dominated by corporate lobbying interests. In such contexts, law functions less as a shield protecting the vulnerable or promoting collective well-being, and more as a shill, an active enabler of entrenched systemic interests and inequalities (The Real

WORLD PEACE

News Network [TRNN], 2018d; ProPublica, 2019; Wakefield, 2018).

Conclusion: Toward Truth, or Die in Fiction

The pattern that emerges from a critical examination of modern legal systems is unmistakably clear: law operates paradoxically as both the purported engine of human progress and enlightenment, and simultaneously as a shackle that binds humanity to its most damaging and self-perpetuating fictions. The true tragedy is not merely that these legal frameworks propagate falsehoods or distortions, but rather that they demand universal complicity—requiring all individuals and societies to participate in and sustain these illusions as if they were immutable truths (Bastiat, 1850/2013; Aeon, 2018e).

Addressing this systemic predicament will not be achieved by layering upon existing frameworks further technical refinements, such as more complex clauses, elaborated protocols, or ostensibly "rational" procedural enhancements. These incremental adjustments only serve to deepen the entrenchment of legal fiction, further obscuring the fundamental nature of law and its role as an instrument of power. Rather, what is urgently required is a collective awakening—a wide-scale recognition and rejection of the law, not as a neutral or benevolent institution, but as an organized system of fiction meticulously constructed to benefit and perpetuate entrenched interests and hierarchies.

True liberation—collective emancipation from these systemic illusions—will be attainable only when individuals and communities as a whole refuse to be either passive audiences or willing actors in these ritualistic abstractions. It demands an insistence that laws be conceived, articulated, and enforced with the primary purpose of serving human needs, dignity, and flourishing, rather than protecting impersonal, abstract systems or ideological constructs. Law must be reclaimed to serve life itself, not serve as a tool of ideological domination. Only through this paradigmatic shift can we hope to transcend the pervasive crimes, injustices, and miseries that the institutionalization of fiction has made normative.

Chapter 8: The Business of Suffering

Business

Throughout human history, societies have always established systems of exchange to facilitate the distribution of goods and services. However, with the emergence and consolidation of modern capitalism, the business model underwent a profound transformation. It evolved from a simple mechanism focused primarily on fulfilling basic human needs into a complex, systematic process aimed at exploiting human wants, desires, and vulnerabilities on a large scale. One of the pivotal legal innovations fueling this transformation was the creation of the joint-stock company (Wikipedia, n.d.-a). This legal form enabled enterprises to pool capital from numerous investors, thus allowing ventures to grow beyond the financial capacity and lifespan of any single individual. Alongside this, the proliferation of early corporations (Wikipedia, n.d.-b) as artificial entities institutionalized the pursuit of profit as an enduring objective, formalizing the endless drive for economic gain across generations.

These corporations—impersonal, non-living legal entities—became the quintessential vehicles for aggregating vast resources, mitigating risks associated with business ventures, and systematically extracting value over extended periods (The Corporation, n.d.; IMDb, n.d.). This shift facilitated not only the growth of businesses but also the expansion of capitalism's reach into practically every aspect of life.

In contemporary society, the boundary between business and personal identity has largely dissolved. The rise of "personal branding" has transformed individuals into products themselves, simultaneously serving as both producers and markets within the economy (BBC, 2017a). This phenomenon illustrates how the marketplace extends its control beyond mere labor and creativity to encompass our innermost anxieties, aspirations, and social identities. Basic human desires—such as health, security, and social belonging—that once existed largely outside formal markets, are now commodified and transformed into transactional relationships. This commodification is evident in innovations like Sweden's cashless economy, which pushes the limits of technological integration and requires elevated levels of social trust (Savage, 2017). Conversely, regions experiencing rapid technological automation face "retail apocalypse," where traditional employment and the social fabric of communities are profoundly destabilized by economic shifts (Levinson-King, 2018).

A critical but often neglected truth about business as a system is that it does not merely serve pre-existing human needs. Rather, it actively shapes and cultivates these needs and wants, strategically creating scarcity, dependence, and consumer desire in ways that ensure continuous profit generation. This dynamic is not confined to consumer goods; it also influences large-scale, collective projects. Mega-infrastructure endeavors and the nascent commercialization of space exploration are prime examples of ambitions coordinated and enabled by the organizational and financial power of the corporate form (BBC, 2017b; BBC, 2017c). However, the underlying motivations driving these projects frequently diverge starkly from the public narratives of progress, innovation, and common good that companies often espouse (Aeon, 2017a). Tasioulas (2017) highlights how legal systems designed to protect rights can, paradoxically, be transformed into mechanisms that perpetuate exclusion, control, and commodification rather than fostering genuine emancipation and justice. Hence, world peace is a matter of simply fixing that by enforcing the letter of the law once again.

While the business ecosystem has undeniably accelerated innovation and economic growth, it has also been a significant contributor to persistent social and economic inequalities (Therealnews, n.d.). economic growth for instance causes inflation in every currency. So does population growth. So does anything requiring more currency to be printed. It engineers widespread insecurity and systematically designs dependencies that convert human misery and vulnerability, as well as fulfillment and prosperity, into sources of profit (ProPublica, n.d.-a). See the practice of district "redlining" for any examples of that. The immense power wielded by business leaders—often idolized and celebrated—rarely faces sufficient scrutiny or accountability (Aeon, 2017b). This imbalance further reinforces the prevailing belief that economic success inherently justifies and absolves all repercussions of corporate actions. Consequently, modern society has normalized and institutionalized the idea that widespread misery is not an anomaly but a structural byproduct of the economic system—a phenomenon that is managed, marketed, and sustained to maximize corporate profit (Aeon, 2017c). Hence, abolish money. Business doesn't go away just because money does. The economy remains unchanged except that that "doing the needful things" is the only currency of any reward. It's not like we're not doing everything we need today, anyway. We'll just do it as volunteers once money is gone. And, our species becomes generalists again, sustainability of resources is achieved, and Earth is made habitable for whatever succeeds us.

WORLD PEACE

The Business of War

Historically, war has often been portrayed as a tragic and regrettable consequence of failed diplomacy, ideological clashes, or unavoidable geopolitical tensions. However, in the contemporary global landscape, war has become deeply enmeshed within the global economy, functioning as an exceptionally lucrative enterprise. This entanglement is embodied in what is commonly known as the "military-industrial complex," a term originally coined to caution against the risks of close cooperation between military and industrial sectors, warning how it might unduly influence national policy. Today, this complex is a vast, multifaceted network encompassing defense contractor, private security firms, advanced technology companies, logistics providers, and other associated entities, all interconnected and profiting from perpetual military engagements (Therealnews, n.d.-a).

The scale of this economic powerhouse is staggering, with the U.S. military budget alone exceeding those of many countries combined. This colossal spending funnels billions of dollars annually to private companies involved in everything from weapons manufacturing and surveillance technology to infrastructure reconstruction and logistical support for military operations around the world (ICIJ, n.d.-a). These investments extend far beyond conventional arms production to include emerging technologies critical to modern warfare and security.

Modern conflicts have evolved in character; they are no longer primarily about territorial conquest or purely ideological battles. Instead, they often revolve around securing strategic markets, controlling vital resources such as oil and minerals, and gaining political leverage for transnational corporations and geopolitical interests. The

WORLD PEACE

post-conflict reconstruction of war-torn regions illustrates this dynamic clearly, as it tends to channel immense sums of money into a select group of firms that profit from rebuilding efforts, often with little regard for the social and economic well-being of the affected populations (ICIJ, n.d.-b). In many cases, war is far from accidental; its ongoing persistence is frequently a deliberate outcome of policy decisions designed to maintain conditions favorable to these vested interests. These stakeholders rely on the continuation of conflict for their financial survival and political power (Therealnews, n.d.-b).

Public narratives that shape popular understanding and consent for these wars are carefully managed through media channels and political discourse. These narratives turn civilian populations into willing consumers of security measures and militarized solutions, reinforcing support for sustained and often escalating military spending. Yet, this spending rarely results in durable peace, instead perpetuating cycles of violence and instability (BBC, 2018).

Notably, major corporations have repeatedly profited from humanitarian crises, securing lucrative contracts not only during active conflicts but also in their aftermath. These contracts involve rebuilding destroyed infrastructure, managing refugee and displacement crises, or establishing comprehensive surveillance regimes under the guise of security—a practice often justified through fear and uncertainty (BBC, 2017d). The modern "merchants of death" encompass far more than traditional arms dealers; they include data brokers, information technology firms, private military contractors, and media conglomerates, all of whom extract economic value from continuing disorder and insecurity (Therealnews, n.d.-a).

WORLD PEACE

Even in moments when peace appears attainable, the entrenched machinery of war actively works to justify its existence and continued funding. The phenomenon of "forever wars," where military engagements drag on indefinitely, generates steady financial returns for investors at the cost of prolonged suffering and devastation for countless civilian populations caught in the crossfire (Military.com, 2020; Wikipedia, n.d.-c).

Furthermore, many of the technological advancements initially developed for wartime applications, such as sophisticated surveillance systems or artificial intelligence-driven cyber operations, frequently transition into peacetime use. These technologies often expand the commodification of global insecurities, enabling governments and private actors to monitor, control, and profit from a wide range of societal anxieties beyond the battlefield (BBC, 2017e). In this sense, the business of war is not a breakdown or failure of civilization; rather, it constitutes a core and deliberate component of the prevailing economic and political ideology in the contemporary world.

The Business of Misery

Business does not merely profit from war; it systematically capitalizes on all forms of human suffering, often structuring both the origins and responses to crises in ways that maximize financial returns. One of the most striking and pervasive examples of this phenomenon is found within the healthcare industry. Powerful pharmaceutical corporations routinely allocate significantly more resources to marketing and advertising than to the fundamental research and development of new medicines. This prioritization fosters widespread dependence on costly, often symptom-focused medical solutions, while frequently neglecting—or in some

WORLD PEACE

cases exacerbating—the underlying causes of disease and poor health (Washington Post, 2015; Statista, n.d.). This approach sustains a cycle wherein patients become dependent on expensive treatments without addressing preventive care or social determinants of health. And all this process is fine. Medicine as a discipline evolves like anything else. But self-preservation is a human right. And, nothing stands in the way of human rights. Certainly not the evolution of a business.

The deep disparities in healthcare access and outcomes across different populations are not incidental but are rather maintained by deliberate policy decisions. These policies ensure that only a privileged subset of society can afford the highest standards of medical care, whether in the management of chronic diseases, the fight against epidemics, or the provision of mental health support (CNN, 2017a). Such inequalities help preserve lucrative markets for private healthcare providers and pharmaceutical companies, reinforcing barriers to equitable health access. This certainly qualifies as crimes against humanity.

Similarly, environmental crises—including widespread pollution, unsafe drinking water, and industrial disasters—are often perpetuated by corporate actors that externalize the costs of environmental degradation onto vulnerable communities. These businesses subsequently market solutions as value-added products or services, turning the remediation of problems they contributed to into profitable ventures (UNICEF, 2017; BBC, 2017f). Populations most affected by environmental harms—such as children exposed to severe pollution, communities devastated by famine, or those grappling with pandemics and opioid dependency—are increasingly commodified as captive "markets" for pharmaceuticals, health insurance, and charitable donations (ProPublica, n.d.-b; CNN, 2017b).

Even humanitarian relief and aid efforts operate within complex economic ecosystems where charities, contractors, and governmental bodies all hold vested financial interests. While these efforts are framed as altruistic, they often foster dependency rather than solve foundational issues by creating cycles reliant on continuous inflows of aid money and resources (CNN, 2017b). True, unrequited, altruism is a virtue completely repressed in humans today by money.

The prevalence of misery in society, therefore, is neither an abnormal occurrence nor a simple consequence of misfortune. Instead, it is actively designed and manufactured through mechanisms such as regulatory capture, systemic labor exploitation, and the deliberate under-provision of essential public goods like healthcare, education, and housing (Aeon, 2017d; BBC, 2017g). Financial crises further exemplify this dynamic, transforming widespread human suffering into profitable opportunities through predatory lending practices, the commodification of bankruptcy, and through the speculative activities of global capital markets (ProPublica, n.d.-a).

This interrelationship between structured misery and economic incentives is evident in findings such as those in the World Happiness Report (2018), which identifies those countries marked by high economic inequality and limited access to fundamental services—such as health and education—experience persistent social unhappiness. This correlation highlights the direct and damaging impact of profit-driven business models on collective well-being.

WORLD PEACE

In these contexts, purported "solutions" to social and economic suffering rarely aim to eliminate the root causes of distress. Instead, they focus on managing misery in a way that is financially sustainable and profitable. These approaches often provide partial, costly reliefs that do not fundamentally alter the underlying structures that generate suffering (Aeon, 2017e; Therealnews, n.d.-c). Thus, the business of misery creates and sustains a self-perpetuating market in which pain, poverty, and insecurity are as valuable—if not more so—than health, well-being, or prosperity ever could be. This cycle ensures that human suffering remains an integral and profitable component of contemporary capitalist economies. The relentless pursuit and acquisition of money at all costs and everything having a price tag, therefore, constitutes crimes against humanity.

Chapter 9: Politics, Power, and Global Influence

Politics

Politics, by its very nature and design, serves as the foundational mechanism through which power is distributed, exercised, and justified within societies. Ideally, politics should embody the principles of collective governance and pursuit of the public good, ensuring that decisions are made in the interest of the many rather than the few. However, these ideals have frequently been undermined or outright co-opted by entrenched powerful interests—whether political elites, wealthy individuals, or corporate entities—whose primary objectives often revolve around advancing their own self-serving agendas. This profound disconnect between political rhetoric and reality has fueled widespread disillusionment and a decline in public confidence across the globe. The pervasive erosion of trust is symbolized by an ongoing series of scandals, chronic institutional gridlock, and the normalization of corruption as a routine political practice. One stark illustration of such systemic corruption is found in revelations about Azerbaijan's use of an opaque $3 billion slush fund, strategically deployed to buy international influence and obscure authoritarian abuses within its borders (BBC News, 2017). It is why the majority of humans don't do the politics ideology.

The entanglement of political power with big business creates an additional and deeply corrosive dimension to this crisis of legitimacy. Rather than serving as separate arms of governance and enterprise, political parties and corporations frequently operate in a closely intertwined manner. Political parties often act as agents delivering legislation favorable to corporate interests, while corporations reciprocate by providing substantial campaign financing, lobbying efforts, and lucrative post-public-office positions—commonly referred to as sinecures—for influential politicians once their official terms end (Reclaim Democracy, n.d.-a). This symbiosis not only undermines democratic accountability but also hollow out substantive democratic governance. This erosion of genuine political competition is evident in specific phenomena such as the staging of presidential debates, where corporate interests frequently control the format and content to ensure sanitized, scripted encounters rather than authentic, open civic discourse (Reclaim Democracy, n.d.-b).

In many Western democracies, the rise of populism exemplifies another tool through which political elites manipulate power dynamics to their advantage. Although historically populism mobilized working-class movements toward emancipatory political change, its contemporary usage often centers on divisions along ethnic, nationalist, and xenophobic lines. This strategic deployment of "manufactured division" diverts political energy away from pursuing material improvements and redistributive justice, instead channeling popular frustration into symbolic culture wars. As a result, true political power remains ignored by the majority, while the minority electorate becomes fragmented and distracted by superficial battles over identity and symbolism rather than engagement in the structural shaping of economic and social outcomes (Aeon, 2019a; Aeon, 2018a).

Beyond this, the increasing capture of political processes by media conglomerates, big technology companies, and other vested interests further distorts democratic functioning. These powerful actors control information flows and manipulate public discourse to shape electoral outcomes and policy debates in ways that serve their own commercial or ideological goals. Consequently, many citizens question not only the legitimacy of elections but also the authenticity of their political representation, fostering widespread skepticism about whether elected officials truly act on behalf of the public (Hemingway, 2021). This pervasive climate of distrust and disenchantment has contributed to declining hope in the political system. Such disenchantment, in turn, fuels the rise of authoritarian and illiberal regimes, which capitalize on cynicism and political disengagement to consolidate power and undermine democratic institutions (Aeon, 2017).

Governance

Governance, in its original conception, represented the structured and principled effort to direct and manage public affairs with integrity, transparency, and rationality. Humans manage governance exceptionally well, as do many other organisms in the natural world. After a population size of 440 or so, humans demonstrate wanderlust to produce a separate population. These populations tribe. Multiple tribes for nations under a nationalist identity. And multiple nations crowed. It is only through the formalized government structure that humans exceeded that 440-individual inclination of our species to form mega sized countries predicated on politics.

WORLD PEACE

Government embodied the ideal of serving the common good through effective institutions, inclusive decision-making, and equitable resource allocation. However, in contemporary political contexts, governance increasingly finds itself captured or systematically undermined by the very political forces it was intended to rise above. Governance is never government. This capture manifests in the form of entrenched interests, corruption, and procedural dysfunction that erode the ability of governments to function impartially or effectively.

The United States stands as a prominent example of these challenges, where fundamental design flaws within governmental structures and mechanisms have contributed to persistent policy failures. These failures include an inability to adequately address critical social needs such as healthcare, affordable housing, education, and infrastructure development. This dysfunction has fueled debates among scholars, commentators, and policymakers about whether the U.S. exhibits characteristics of a "failed state," a label traditionally reserved for countries where governance collapses completely or where the rule of law and basic services are absent (Aeon, 2020a; Wikipedia, n.d.-a). While the United States is far from such an extreme, the repeated polarization, legislative gridlock, and institutional paralysis reveal significant weaknesses in governance capacity.

Elsewhere, the phenomenon of political deadlock similarly highlights governance challenges, as illustrated by countries like Italy, where protracted political crises and unstable coalition governments frequently undermine effective policymaking. Such circumstances regularly provoke volatility in financial markets, which react with panic to political uncertainty, demonstrating how governance is often subject to the whims of short-term political tactics rather than guided by coherent, long-term strategies oriented toward the welfare of the broader population (BBC News, 2018).

A comprehensive global survey of governance reveals a complex landscape marked by varying degrees of success and failure. Countries that maintain stable, transparent, and accountable institutions consistently outperform those where political interference, systemic corruption, and bureaucratic inefficiency predominate (BBC, 2018a; Wikipedia, n.d.-b). Strong governance frameworks tend to correlate with higher levels of economic development, social stability, and citizen trust. Yet, even in nations widely regarded as having some of the "best-governed" systems, marginalized and vulnerable communities frequently remain politically and economically disenfranchised by policies of country. This persistent exclusion underscores that the mere existence of formal structures and institutions is insufficient to guarantee justice, inclusion, or equal participation even in well-managed governance, and rarely, if ever, in government.

Governance is a condition of the human existence. Yet, there is nothing natural about government, and it must be foisted upon the population. The inherent complexity, opacity, and hierarchical nature of government institutions obfuscate the reality of minority rule, worldwide, but also serve to shield elites from meaningful accountability. Legal immunities granted to public officials, coupled with protected salaries and benefits, contribute to a self-reinforcing system wherein those in positions of power become increasingly insulated from popular oversight and consequence. This detachment from democratic responsiveness creates a governance dynamic in which public officials may prioritize their own privileges or the interests of narrow powerful groups over the needs and demands of the citizenry they ostensibly serve (Murse, 2020; The Conversation, 2018). Within such systems, politics and governance cease to operate as mechanisms of problem-solving or equitable resource management. Instead, they become tools for perpetuating social divisions, reinforcing privilege, and maintaining established power structures rather than addressing or resolving underlying societal grievances.

Nationalism

If politics can be understood as the grand theater within which power is distributed and contested, then nationalism serves as one of its most potent and enduring scripts. Potent because it reflects the natural order of human cooperation and congregation. Enduring because that has been the single source of human endurance, perseverance, and longevity over 250,000 years. In the contemporary era, nationalism has experienced a pronounced resurgence, but in an ideological connotation, widely recognized as an exclusionary and often divisive ideology that pits communities against one another along lines of race, religion, ethnicity, and culture. Interesting how truth and accuracy are different things, and politics are masters of manipulators of both, or either, in the interest of divisiveness, or simple obfuscation of reality. Get them asking the wrong questions, and you needn't worry about the answers, as they say.

The manipulation is typically linguistic in nature. Since human language and conversation are so inadequate to the task of effective communication, linguistic legerdemain is

WORLD PEACE

the most effective tool of media, ideology, and/or theology. First you own the word, then you own its meaning. So, while nationalism has nothing to do with politics, the framed story about nationalism is that though nationalism was originally forged as a tool for collective self-determination—enabling oppressed or marginalized groups to assert their rights and identities—the ideology has increasingly come to serve darker and more regressive purposes. Today, nationalism frequently props up what Aeon (2018b) terms "cruel moralisers," political actors who cloak themselves in a "halo" of virtuous and righteous rhetoric while simultaneously perpetuating entrenched systems of exclusion, discrimination, and inequality.

This re-emergence of nationalist sentiment has been particularly evident in the heartlands of Europe and in the United States, where populist figures and movements have successfully tapped into historical grievances, economic dislocations, and cultural anxieties. And, every one of those are political, with their own unique ideological bents, in the US, at least. These leaders and organizations stoke fears by warning of external threats—whether immigration, globalization, or perceived foreign enemies—while diverting public attention from profound internal inequalities and systemic social problems (Hill, 2018; PBS NewsHour, 2017a). The language deployed in these nationalist discourses frequently centers on a stark dichotomy of "good versus evil," casting the nation and its purported "true" citizens as virtuous defenders against nefarious outsiders. This rhetoric masterfully draws sharp, often hostile borders not only around geographic territory but also around collective identity, belonging, and the parameters of who is considered worthy of inclusion (Aeon,

2018c). Yet, in its original inception and for hundreds of thousands of years, nationalism was how tribal humans congregated, and that was all inclusive.

One revealing manifestation of nationalism's commodification lies in the emergence and proliferation of citizenship-for-sale programs. These programs offer wealthy individuals the opportunity to acquire formal national citizenships through financial investment, a practice that lays bare the market logic underpinning even the most sacred and historically significant national boundaries. You'll see this practiced in many countries across the globe. This commodification transforms nationality from a deeply rooted cultural and, today, political identity into a transactional good, further complicating questions of belonging and sovereignty (BBC News, 2017b). The US, of course, does not participate since it remains the only country in the Americas where citizenship is free.

The more malevolent aspects of today's political nationalism are also systematically sustained and exacerbated by the modern media ecosystem and online platforms, where hate speech, conspiracy theories, and inflammatory rhetoric flourish. These digital spaces act as accelerants to ideological nationalist politics, reinforcing narratives of division, exclusion, and repression. The resulting climate can escalate tensions, fuel social polarization and lay the groundwork for outbreaks of violence, ethnic cleansing, or even warfare (BBC News, 2017c; Aeon, 2018d). Instead of fostering international cooperation and solidarity, nationalism's resurgence as political ideology threatens to unravel these efforts, endangering global stability and peace by deepening fractures between nations and peoples.

In sum, while nationalism once served as a force for collective empowerment and self-determination, its contemporary resurgence as ideology reflects a potent political script that enforces division, entrenches privilege, and risks reversing decades of progress toward inclusivity and cooperation in international relations.

Globalization

In stark contrast to the insularity and exclusionary impulses of today's political nationalism, globalization represents a complex and multifaceted process of integration that has woven together economies, cultures, political ideas, and communication networks at an unprecedented global scale. This phenomenon has transformed how societies interact, enabling the rapid movement of goods, services, capital, information, and people across borders. However, globalization is far from a universally positive or inevitable force advancing equity and shared prosperity. Instead, its so-called "devastating success" has primarily enriched a narrow global elite while simultaneously unleashing profound discontent and upheaval among vast populations who experience displacement, marginalization, and socio-economic precarity as direct consequences of integration (Sundaram, 2009a, 2009b, 2009c).

One central driver of globalization has been the systematic dismantling of national barriers that once regulated trade, capital flows, labor mobility, and information exchange. While lowering these barriers has fostered dynamic international markets and innovation, it has also generated significant disruptions at local and national levels. The rapid disappearance of stable manufacturing jobs and other traditional forms of employment, along with the erosion of distinctive local cultures and social structures, has left many communities economically vulnerable and culturally disoriented. These dislocations frequently result in heightened economic inequality within and between countries, fueling political backlash, social fragmentation, and the rise of protectionist and ideologically nationalist political movements seeking to resist or reverse globalization's reach (BBC News, 2017d; Aeon, 2019b).

Moreover, globalization has been adeptly exploited by transnational corporations as a strategic tool to weaken and bypass regulatory frameworks designed to protect workers, the environment, and consumers. Through practices such as regulatory arbitrage—deliberately locating operations in regions with lax labor laws or environmental standards—multinational companies undermine unions, degrade labor rights, and intensify wealth concentration at the very top of the economic pyramid. These dynamics occur under the rhetoric of economic progress and efficiency but often contribute to exploitative practices and social injustice, obscuring the true human and environmental costs of globalized production and finance (ProPublica, n.d.; Therealnews, n.d.-a; Aeon, 2018e).

Despite its many challenges and contradictions, globalization also opens important pathways for positive change and transformative innovation—especially when global ideas are thoughtfully adapted, localized, and reshaped by diverse actors and social movements on the ground. It is how humans operated for 250,000 years successfully prior to "the great burn". Transnational flows of knowledge, technologies, and cultural influences have the potential to inspire new forms of cooperation, human rights advocacy, environmental stewardship, again, and democratic participation, today. Yet, this constructive potential remains contingent on the vitality and resilience of democratic institutions and grassroots solidarities operating within local contexts. And, it is always predicated on majority rule, absent ideology of every type and kind. True global cooperation cannot be reduced simply to the flat, market-driven logic and profit maximization characteristic of multinational corporations; it requires robust social foundations, participatory governance, and equitable decision-making processes that center people and communities rather than capital (Aeon, 2017a; Aeon, 2020b). And, such is the voice of the majority, worldwide, absent ideology.

Ultimately, globalization represents a process marked by deep paradoxes: it connects us more closely than ever before while simultaneously producing winners and losers; it promises innovation and progress yet perpetuates inequalities and vulnerabilities. Understanding and navigating these tensions is essential for forging a more inclusive, just, and sustainable global order in the twenty-first century. Or, just get rid of money and see how easy negotiating all of it becomes again.

Science

For centuries, science has been celebrated as a neutral, objective, and rational pursuit dedicated to uncovering truths about the natural world. It is often regarded as a beacon of enlightenment, progressing independently of cultural biases or political agendas. However, this idealized view glosses over the complex and often fraught relationship between science, politics, and ideology. What's wrong with science being popular, or even profitable? When it's popular; it's politics. When it's profitable, it's a business. And the last thing it is then is science. Barely trustworthy knowledge. Scientific knowledge and institutions are far from immune to the prevailing currents of political power and ideological influence. It's just the way the Scientific Method works; you have to keep testing a theory once it is postulated. Throughout history and continuing into the present day, political regimes have frequently sought to manipulate scientific findings to align with their own strategic objectives, rewriting, suppressing, or distorting evidence in order to validate ideological narratives or policy positions (Perera, 2017; BBC News, 2017e). The business of science requires findings to remain static if funding and ROI are to be calculable and predictable, so the "science" being funded never progresses, and touted as "settled science". Politics requires that science remain fluid in order to maintain and promote the changing winds of ideological bent.

Even in ostensibly open and democratic societies, the allocation of research funding frequently reflects political priorities and vested interests. Funding bodies and governments may direct resources to support studies likely to produce preferred outcomes, marginalizing or discrediting research that challenges dominant paradigms or threatens powerful stakeholders. In this instrumentalized context, science can become an "ideological weapon" deployed in policy disputes to bolster particular agendas while undermining competing views, rather than a disinterested pursuit of knowledge (BBC News, 2017f).

Science has also been co-opted as a vehicle for partizan nationalist and ideological narratives. Historic scientific achievements are often selectively emphasized or reinterpreted to bolster national pride, portraying scientific progress as a marker of national superiority or cultural ascendancy. Messages to be reiterated by wrote, as if a stage play. Conversely, inconvenient scientific facts—especially those tied to globally pressing issues such as climate change, environmental degradation, or infectious disease outbreaks—are frequently suppressed, trivialized, or reframed to minimize political fallout or economic consequences (CNN, 2017; BBC News, 2017g). This selective valorization distorts public understanding of science and undermines the basis for informed decision-making on critical global challenges.

Simultaneously, the increasing integration of scientific research with commercial interests and political power structures has redefined the social role of expertise. Scientific expertise is often valorized and amplified only when it supports the prevailing interests of those in power. This dynamic narrow the range of legitimate scientific voices and perspectives, privileging technical knowledge that maintains existing hierarchies and marginalizing dissenting or alternative approaches (Aeon, 2019c).

The co-optation of science thus plays a decisive role not only in sustaining social and political divisions but also in rationalizing practices of repression, militarization, and authoritarian governance. Scientific discourse and institutions can be mobilized to justify war, surveillance, and other forms of state violence under the guise of rational necessity or security imperatives (Aeon, 2019d). This troubling reality helps explain why, in recent years, scientific "consensus" itself has become a target of public distrust and

WORLD PEACE

orchestrated misinformation campaigns. As the popular ideological story would have it; efforts to sow doubt, confusion, and skepticism regarding well-established scientific facts—whether in climate science, vaccination, or other areas—reflect deliberate strategies aimed at undermining the authority of science and weakening policy responses to urgent problems (Bloomberg, 2018).

In summary, while science retains enormous potential as a transformative and clarifying force, it exists within a complex terrain deeply shaped by political and economic power. Its purported neutrality is frequently compromised by ideological agendas and vested interests. Recognizing and addressing these tensions is essential for restoring science's credibility, ensuring its integrity, and harnessing its potential to contribute meaningfully to social progress and global well-being. Abolish money, and that is accomplished. Not to mention restoring our human right to trustworthy knowledge.

Part IV

What are you willing to commit to

Chapter 10: The Path Forward and the Role of Choice

As this book draws to its conclusion, the focus of the narrative shifts away from merely uncovering and exposing the deep-rooted causes of injustice, inequality, and conflict that permeate the global as the system of all human misery. Instead, it moves toward addressing the most vital and urgent question facing us all: **What are you willing to commit to** in the pursuit of a more just and peaceful world? It's as simple as an email to the POICC. Literally. This shift emphasizes the importance of individual and collective responsibility, urging the majority and the minority, alike, to recognize their own agency as active participants rather than passive observers of ongoing social and political dynamics. Humans run this planet, not ideology.

The path to world peace, contrary to popular belief, is not an elusive or inscrutable mystery reserved for diplomats or statespersons. It is, at its core, a deliberate and conscious collective decision that requires sustained engagement, empathy, and commitment from ordinary individuals as well as from communities and institutions. It is, at its most fundamental, up to us, as a species. Achieving such peace demands that we move beyond resignation or cynicism and instead mobilize our capacities for solidarity, dialogue, and constructive action, recognizing that no lasting transformation can occur without broad participation. It is the way to virtue, honor, nobility, wisdom, and imagination again; qualities of Man unrecognized by our species, in their full majesty, for 13,000 years.

This intentional commitment entails acknowledging the interconnectedness of global challenges—from economic disparities and environmental degradation to political polarization and cultural conflict—and embracing the role each person can play in addressing them. A simple letter writing campaign. World peace has never been so easily achieved. Just voice your desire for it. Even reference this book, if you like. The POICC are very well aware, and expecting your correspondences.

Peace Is Possible—and Simple

History offers ample evidence that the infusion of ideology into the natural tendencies of humans to adapt and overcome persistent evolutionary challenges have, over millennia, contributed to vast cycles of conflict, widespread human misery, and profound environmental degradation (Burl Minnis, 2025). These systems—whether based on hierarchies of wealth, politics, power, or celebrity—are not natural or inevitable; rather, they represent artificial constructs, products of human imagination and collective consent. But the majority have never consented. So, we're just fixing that. And, all the laws necessary are already on the books. Now, it's just your turn to join the majority, or not. Your choice, no obligations. The authority and influence of those so elevated by the minority, worldwide, while deeply entrenched in perceptions of reality, depend fundamentally on the continuation of ideology and perpetual buffooning along with the rules they impose. If these structures are artificial, so too is their power—abolish money and the very impetus for their existence disappears.

The solution to the crises that define much of human history and contemporary existence is, astonishingly, remarkably simple and fundamentally accessible to all: humanity can consciously choose to set aside all organized ideological frameworks that perpetuate competition, greed, narcissism, and division, and return to the virtues that are the best qualities of our species, naturally, without the crushing repression of fiction. This is not mere wishful thinking or idealistic fantasy; it is a rational, deliberate, and actionable strategy grounded in the power of collective human agency, and perhaps you last best chance for world peace. And, all the legal and political mechanisms are already in place just waiting on your voice.

Imagine a world in which individuals, collectively and decisively, abandon the systems that enforce economic disparities, social hierarchies, and destructive rivalries— systems that have long incentivized exploitation, alienation, and environmental plunder. By actually, physically setting all "general ledgers" of the world to zero world peace results. Such a fundamental repair to the process of rational human reason would free the species from the repressing constraints of ideology on rational right actions and allow our species to once again enjoy our highest qualities of virtue, honor, nobility, wisdom, and imagination.

And, nothing changes for Man in the way we do anything. Everything we did yesterday with money, we will do tomorrow without money the same way. Ideology never solved anything. We were just made to believe it does. It's just how all ideology has always worked since monetary economy emerged in this system of all human misery.

A Call to Action

I can't obligate you to this liberation of our species. You have to do it, or not do it, but make that decision because it's what you want to do. I've laid it all out for you here in no uncertain terms. It is irrefutable and undeniable. Awareness alone, while vital, is insufficient to effect the transformative

WORLD PEACE

changes so urgently needed. Writing to the International Criminal Court (ICC) serves that objective. Have the simply pick a day, take that date to the NU, and within minutes – literally – the world can be at peace, and no one needs to die, and nothing changes in the way Man does anything.

The urgency of this call to action cannot be overstated. Around the globe, current crises place unprecedented strains on human populations and the natural world alike. According to data from the United Nations High Commissioner for Refugees (UNHCR), nearly 71 million people were forcibly displaced within a single year as a result of war, persecution, political instability, and other forms of violence and hardship (UNHCR, as cited in Schmitz, 2019). These staggering numbers represent millions of lives uprooted and trajectories of community destabilization that ripple far beyond their immediate contexts.

Compounding these humanitarian crises are accelerating environmental emergencies, which exacerbate threats to both human and nonhuman life. Entire ecosystems face catastrophic collapse—from the alarming and well-documented mass die-offs of honey bee populations, critical pollinators essential to global food systems (Charles, 2019), to the silent, pervasive extinction events threatening countless species and biomes across continents. These ecological emergencies are inextricably linked to human activity and monetary economic systems. Can't have war without politics, can't have trash without money.

Humanity is far from exempt from these cascading threats; on the contrary, our current social and environmental trajectories put not only the planet's biodiversity but also human survival itself at grave risk. Failure to act decisively and collectively risks deepening these crises, whereas urgent solidarity and informed engagement can help forge pathways toward healing, resilience, and a sustainable coexistence with the natural world. But no one needs to die. We all just snap out of it together.

In light of this sobering reality, this work serves as both a moral imperative and a glimmer of hope—inviting every individual to participate in shaping a future defined by peace, justice, and sustainability. Then, we will collectively rise to the level of human greatness imagined by our species for generations, to meet the challenges of our last thousand years, as the final iteration in the family of Man, siblings one and all.

Thought Experiments and Examples

What if, as a collective human species, we were to wake up tomorrow with a shared commitment to set aside blame, ideological divisions, and entrenched grievances, and instead choose rational, reasonable right actions, as siblings? While such a shift would not erase suffering. We have – all of us – endured. Pain and injustice are deeply embedded and complex for anyone having lived for any time at all. The intricate economic and political systems that rely on division, competition, and exploitation to maintain power would lose their foundational legitimacy and capacity to sustain conflict.

If any generation will have a hard time with this, it will be ours. And, when I says 'ours' I mean anyone alive today over the age of 5 years old. Greed is not a natural expression. But it is, now, a conation of human experience. Even from the age of 5. Imagine if every person regarded others not as strangers or adversaries, but as members of a vast extended family—our evolutionary siblings bound by a common ancestry. This perspective is grounded in a biological truth: humanity shares collective origins, interlinked fates, and overlapping needs. Everyone alive, today, everywhere, for the last 150 years, is related to everyone else, and that is for the rest of time. It's why we're extinct. We are all born of the same mother and father, now. There is no difference. Whether someone is displaced by war, grappling with the grief of losing their home, or mourning the destruction of a local ecosystem, our experiences root together in shared vulnerability and interdependence (Burl Minnis, 2025; Schmitz, 2019; Charles, 2019). Recognizing this familial bond could foster empathy and solidarity that transcend surface-level differences and political narratives, grounding human relations in a deeper sense of responsibility and care. For my part; I got you.

The Role of Collective Will

Peace, therefore, should be understood not merely as the absence or cessation of overt violence and conflict. It encompasses a far deeper and more comprehensive process: the dismantling and removal of every structural and psychological underpinning that fuels greed, and the relentless want for more that has characterized much of human history for 13,000 years. True peace is an active affirmation and celebration of life in all its forms—both human and nonhuman—recognized and respected on its own intrinsic terms. This vision of peace demands that our societies be guided not by artificial systems of accounting, competition, or rigid ideological frameworks, but by principles rooted in justice, compassion, care, and sustainability.

Burl Minnis

WORLD PEACE

Our collective story as a species, marked by growth, innovation, and also profound contradiction, need not culminate in irreversible devastation. Instead, we have the capacity to consciously end the pernicious ideologies that currently threaten not only our persistence but also that of countless other living beings sharing this planet. This marks a pivotal call to evolve beyond the divisive narratives and artificial constructs that have long perpetuated cycles of violence, exclusion, and environmental degradation.

Intriguingly, the enigmatic absence of evidence for other intelligent civilizations elsewhere in the universe—as noted by observations and reports such as those referenced by Fox News (2019) for instance—may provide a sobering caution rather than simply an unexplained cosmic mystery. This phenomenon, often referred to as the Fermi Paradox, might suggest that advanced life, despite its potential for remarkable achievement, is inherently fleeting. One possible reason for this transience is that technologically and intellectually sophisticated civilizations may often be undone by their own internally generated "fictions": ideologies, systems, and false narratives that distort perception, fuel self-destruction, and ultimately prevent sustainable achievement. And, that is exactly and precisely what happened to us. There is no saving us now. There is no pulling out of this extinction. But we can still decide how we want to go out.

This insight lends profound urgency to the role of collective will in shaping our future. It underscores that peace and survival demand more than isolated actions or hopeful aspirations—they require a fundamental, shared transformation grounded in collective consciousness and coordinated effort. The POICC is set up for exactly that. And, it has always been that way since the Rome Statute was ratified in 2002. Only through the deliberate and unified assertion of values that reject domination, inequality, and exploitation can humanity transcend the perilous patterns threatening both planetary health and species continuity. Just tell them that you are in the majority, and that you demand the use of monetary economy be considered a crime against humanity, and by extension war crimes as well, and that you want to abolish money immediately as the solution to the system of all human misery. In this light, the responsibility rests with each individual to contribute actively in realizing a world where justice, care, and interconnectedness prevail over conflict and division.

Your Commitment Shapes Our Future

The commitment that each reader makes—while deeply personal and individual—resonates with profound global significance. Contribute your voice to this effort, or don't. Every act of engagement, every voice raised in demand for peace, justice, and equity contributes to shaping the collective trajectory of humanity and the planet. It is through this accumulation of individual commitments that the foundations for systemic change are laid. Each person's decision to challenge and refuse the destructive narratives and ideologies that rely on human suffering and environmental degradation as their driving forces becomes an essential part of a larger movement toward transformation.

This commitment transcends passive agreement or abstract hope; it calls for active participation in reshaping social, economic, and political realities. It means standing against systems and beliefs that perpetuate inequality, violence, and ecological harm, and instead advocating for frameworks grounded in care, inclusivity, and sustainable coexistence.

WORLD PEACE

We were successful as a species for over 200,000 years that way. In doing so, individuals not only affirm their own values but also help cultivate a culture in which peace and mutual respect become the normative foundations of human interaction when absent ideologies of every type and kind.

Appendix

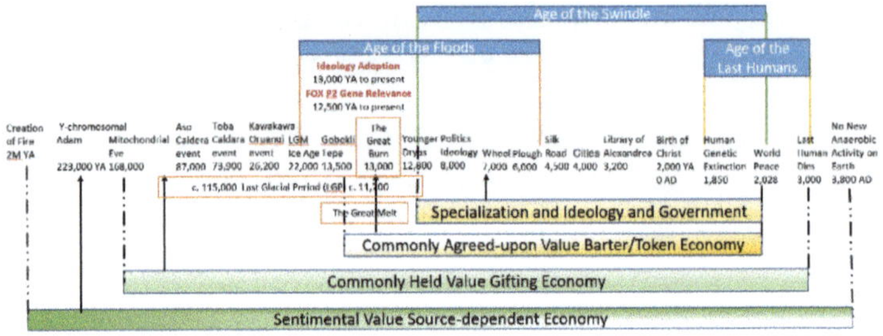

Figure 1

Time table of Potential Events

Table A-10. Reported Registration Rates of Total Voting-Age Population in Presidential Election Years, by Selected Characteristics: November 1968 to 2020

https://www.census.gov/data/tables/time-series/demo/voting-and-registration/voting-historical-time-series.html

(Numbers in thousands)

Characteristic	2022	2020	2016	2012	2008	2004	2000	1996	1992	1988	1984	1980	1976	1972	1968
United States	PROJECTED														
Total Citizen Population	338,297,857	335,942,003	322,940,000	313,830,000	304,090,000	292,810,000	282,160,000	269,390,000	256,510,000	244,500,000	235,820,000	227,220,000	218,040,000	209,900,000	200,710,000
Total, voting age	262,274,000	252,274,000	245,502,000	235,248,000	225,499,000	215,694,000	202,609,000	193,652,000	185,684,000	178,098,000	169,963,000	157,085,000	146,548,000	136,203,000	116,535,000
Total registered voyers	170,508,000	168,508,000	157,596,000	153,157,000	146,311,000	142,070,000	129,540,000	127,661,000	126,578,000	118,589,000	116,106,000	105,035,000	97,761,000	98,480,000	86,574,000
Percent registered voters	64.9	66.7	64.2	65.1	64.9	65.9	63.9	65.9	68.2	66.6	68.3	66.9	66.7	72.3	74.3
Percent of Total Voter Population	50.3	50.1	48.8	48.8	48.1	48.5	45.9	47.4	49.3	48.5	49.2	46.2	44.8	46.9	43.1
Total voters turned out	161,690,457	159,690,457	136,669,276	129,235,000	131,407,000	122,349,000	105,594,000	96,390,000	104,600,000	91,587,000	92,655,000	86,497,000	81,603,000	77,625,000	73,027,000
Percentage voter turned out	61.6	63.5	55.7	54.9	58.3	56.7	52.1	49.8	56.3	51.4	54.5	55.1	55.7	57.0	62.7
Percent of Total Citizen Population	47.8	47.5	42.3	41.2	43.2	41.8	37.4	35.8	40.8	37.5	39.3	38.1	37.4	37.0	36.4

Figure 2

Illustrated in Figure 2 is the voter turnout for the United States in the 2020 presidential election. This data comes from Table A-10, taken from the US Census Bureau website, with the link also included in the Bibliography. Interestingly, the current Table A-10 on the US Census website no longer includes the header information shown in Figure 2 (I added the total citizen population, the totals row, and a projected column for 2024 for convenience). A link to today's US

WORLD PEACE

Census version is also included in Figure 2 for ease of comparison.

Also absent are the total numbers of citizens who register as ideologues solely for the purpose of fulfilling their civic duty to serve on juries. In the US, jury duty is directly tied to voter registration; there is no alternative requirement for jury service except to register as a voter. Yet, consistently, thirteen and a half million citizens never cast a ballot—they only want to fulfill their jury duty obligations.

Additionally, there are approximately two million children included in the total US citizen numbers who do not have voting representation. While parents naturally have a vested interest in their children's wellbeing, there is no proxy voting; parents vote in their own self-interest. This mechanism is part of why voting works.

Further, nearly two million felons, who are still citizens and part of the majority population, do not have the privilege of voting. Total population numbers, including these groups, are available elsewhere on the US Census website, so those figures must be pieced together for a full picture.

The table in Figure 2 was taken in June 2023. All current Table A-10 data on the US Census website omits these details, which obscures what is presented here in Figure 2. By extension, this omission allows political ideology fiction to appear as reality, as if politics were inherently relevant.

It should be noted, however, that it is not the US Census Bureau's responsibility to police voting or voter turnout data. They are merely the repository for such data and the platform where it is presented. Nonetheless, the bureaucracy effectively runs the country, as the majority of citizens have

WORLD PEACE

chosen to entrust governance to the bureaucracy rather than fill the 519,862 seats at local, state, and federal levels across the executive, legislative, and judiciary branches.

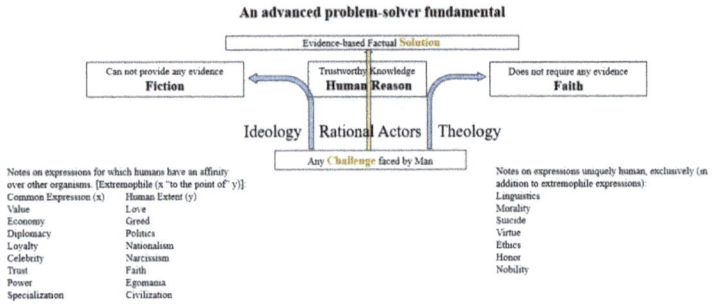

An advanced problem-solver fundamental

Evidence-based Factual Solution

| Can not provide any evidence **Fiction** | Trustworthy Knowledge **Human Reason** | Does not require any evidence **Faith** |

Ideology | Rational Actors | Theology

Any Challenge faced by Man

Notes on expressions for which humans have an affinity over other organisms. [Extremophile (x "to the point of" y)]:

Common Expression (x)	Human Extent (y)
Value	Love
Economy	Greed
Diplomacy	Politics
Loyalty	Nationalism
Celebrity	Narcissism
Trust	Faith
Power	Egomania
Specialization	Civilization

Notes on expressions uniquely human, exclusively (in addition to extremophile expressions):

Linguistics
Morality
Suicide
Virtue
Ethics
Honor
Nobility

Figure 3

Notes on;

Fiction = the willful suspension of disbelief

Ideology = fiction being made, seemingly, real by rule, or tool, or code of law:

Economy

Politics

Bibliography

1. Adams, R. (2021). How archives can make or break a philosopher's reputation. *Aeon*. https://aeon.co/essays/how-archives-can-make-or-break-a-philosophers-reputation

2. Aeon. (2015a). Monopoly was invented to demonstrate the evils of capitalism. https://aeon.co/ideas/monopoly-was-invented-to-demonstrate-the-evils-of-capitalism

3. Aeon. (2015b). How free-market ideology perverts the vocabulary of democracy. https://aeon.co/ideas/how-free-market-ideology-perverts-the-vocabulary-of-democracy

4. Aeon. (2016a). The roots of writing lie in hopes and dreams, not in accounting. https://aeon.co/essays/the-roots-of-writing-lie-in-hopes-and-dreams-not-in-accounting

5. AEON. (2016b). What if jobs are not the solution but the problem. https://aeon.co/essays/what-if-jobs-are-not-the-solution-but-the-problem

6. Aeon. (2016c). Before government cheese was a punchline... https://aeon.co/videos/before-government-cheese-was-a-punchline-it-was-an-experimental-economic-plan

7. Aeon. (2017). *How fetuses learn to talk while they're still in the womb*. https://aeon.co/essays/how-fetuses-learn-to-talk-while-theyre-still-in-the-womb

8. Aeon. (2017a). Populism now divides, yet once it united the working class. https://aeon.co/ideas/populism-now-divides-yet-once-it-united-the-working-class

9. Aeon. (2017b). Children today are suffering a severe deficit of play. https://aeon.co/essays/children-today-are-suffering-a-severe-deficit-of-play

WORLD PEACE

10. Aeon. (2017c). For 97% of human history, equality was the norm. What happened? https://aeon.co/essays/for-97-of-human-history-equality-was-the-norm-what-happened

11. Aeon. (2017d). How ergodicity reimagines economics for the benefit of us all. https://aeon.co/ideas/how-ergodicity-reimagines-economics-for-the-benefit-of-us-all

12. AEON. (2017e). The rule of law and racial difference in the British empire. https://aeon.co/essays/the-rule-of-law-and-racial-difference-in-the-british-empire

13. Aeon. (2017f). When faced with so-called progressive business, stay skeptical. https://aeon.co/ideas/when-faced-with-so-called-progressive-business-stay-skeptical

14. Aeon. (2017g). CEOs should have been the fall guys. Why are they still heroes? https://aeon.co/ideas/ceos-should-have-been-the-fall-guys-why-are-they-still-heroes

15. Aeon. (2017h). Even if you build it, the poor can't come: against supply-side. https://aeon.co/essays/even-if-you-build-it-the-poor-cant-come-against-supply-side

16. Aeon. (2017i). To understand physics, we need to tell and hear stories. https://aeon.co/essays/to-understand-physics-we-need-to-tell-and-hear-stories

17. Aeon. (2017j). What was it like to grow up in the last ice age? https://aeon.co/essays/what-was-it-like-to-grow-up-in-the-last-ice-age

18. AEON. (2017k). Why religious identities are not immune to robust criticism. https://aeon.co/essays/why-religious-identities-are-not-immune-to-robust-criticism

19. Aeon. (2017l). Economic update: Capitalism makes few winners, many losers.

WORLD PEACE

https://therealnews.com/stories/economic-update-capitalism-makes-few-winners-many-losers
20. Aeon. (2017m). How Adam Smith became a surprising hero to conservative economists. https://aeon.co/ideas/how-adam-smith-became-a-surprising-hero-to-conservative-economists
21. Aeon. (2017n). The rift valley tells the entire human story from the start. https://aeon.co/essays/the-rift-valley-tells-the-entire-human-story-from-the-start
22. Aeon. (2017o). Why stoicism is one of the best mind hacks ever devised. https://aeon.co/essays/why-stoicism-is-one-of-the-best-mind-hacks-ever-devised
23. AEON. (2017p). Will medicine ever recover from the perverse economics of drugs. https://aeon.co/essays/will-medicine-ever-recover-from-the-perverse-economics-of-drugs
24. Aeon. (2017q). Is debunking more about the truth-teller than the truth? https://aeon.co/essays/is-debunking-more-about-the-truth-teller-than-the-truth
25. Aeon. (2017r). We need slow hope in a world of accelerating ecological change. https://aeon.co/essays/we-need-slow-hope-in-a-world-of-accelerating-ecological-change
26. Aeon. (2017s). Why one branch on the human family tree replaced all the others. https://aeon.co/essays/why-one-branch-on-the-human-family-tree-replaced-all-the-others
27. Aeon. (2017t). A history of why we hoard, when we store, and who collects. https://aeon.co/essays/a-history-of-why-we-hoard-when-we-store-and-who-collects
28. Aeon. (2017u). Modern culture blames parents for forces beyond their control.

WORLD PEACE

https://aeon.co/essays/modern-culture-blames-parents-for-forces-beyond-their-control

29. Aeon. (2017v). What is the link between medieval and modern antisemitism? https://aeon.co/essays/what-is-the-link-between-medieval-and-modern-antisemitism

30. Aeon. (2017w). Will new drugs mean the rich live to 120 and the poor die at 60? https://aeon.co/essays/will-new-drugs-mean-the-rich-live-to-120-and-the-poor-die-at-60

31. Aeon. (2017x). How changing the metaphors we use can change the way we think. https://aeon.co/essays/how-changing-the-metaphors-we-use-can-change-the-way-we-think

32. Aeon. (2017y). What we're doing when we're doing epistemology. https://aeon.co/essays/what-were-doing-when-were-doing-epistemology

33. Aeon. (2017z). Why longtermism is the world's most dangerous secular credo. https://aeon.co/essays/why-longtermism-is-the-worlds-most-dangerous-secular-credo

34. Aeon. (2017a'a). Think about it: your existence is utterly astonishing. https://aeon.co/essays/think-about-it-your-existence-is-utterly-astonishing

35. Aeon. (2017a'b). For over a century, telepathy has been just around the corner. https://aeon.co/essays/for-over-a-century-telepathy-has-been-just-around-the-corner

36. Aeon. (2017a'c). How Philippa Foot set her mind against prevailing moral philosophy. https://aeon.co/essays/how-philippa-foot-set-her-mind-against-prevailing-moral-philosophy

37. AEON. (2018a). A radical legal ideology nurtured our era of economic inequality.

WORLD PEACE

https://aeon.co/ideas/a-radical-legal-ideology-nurtured-our-era-of-economic-inequality
38. Aeon. (2018b). How do elites manage to hijack voters' ideas of themselves. https://aeon.co/essays/how-do-elites-manage-to-hijack-voters-ideas-of-themselves
39. Aeon. (2018c). Human communities populate the earth. https://www.khanacademy.org/humanities/whp-origins/era-2-early-humans-250000-years-bp-to-3000-bce/2-1-humans-as-a-divergence/a/human-communities-populate-the-earth-beta
40. Aeon. (2018d). 6,000 years ago: Scientists find a Neolithic society treated immigrants as equals. https://www.msn.com/en-us/news/world/6-000-years-ago-scientists-find-a-neolithic-society-treated-immigrants-as-equals/ar-BB1or0xq
41. Aeon. (2018e). How the cruel moraliser uses a halo to disguise his horns. https://aeon.co/essays/how-the-cruel-moraliser-uses-a-halo-to-disguise-his-horns
42. AEON. (201fc). How cold war philosophy permeates US society to this day. https://aeon.co/essays/how-cold-war-philosophy-permeates-us-Society-to-this-day
43. Aeon. (2018g). How did usury stop being a sin and become respectable finance. https://aeon.co/essays/how-did-usury-stop-being-a-sin-and-become-respectable-finance
44. Aeon. (2018h). Why is pop culture obsessed with battles between good and evil. https://aeon.co/essays/why-is-pop-culture-obsessed-with-battles-between-good-and-evil
45. Aeon. (2018i). How the fear of being duped makes you an anxious sucker. https://aeon.co/essays/how-

the-fear-of-being-duped-makes-you-an-anxious-sucker

46. AEON. (2018j). Imre Lakatos and the philosophy of bad science. https://aeon.co/essays/imre-lakatos-and-the-philosophy-of-bad-science

47. Aeon. (2018k). Why some countries come together while others fall apart. https://aeon.co/essays/why-some-countries-come-together-while-others-fall-apart

48. Aeon. (2018l). How ad hominem arguments can demolish appeals to authority. https://aeon.co/ideas/how-ad-hominem-arguments-can-demolish-appeals-to-authority

49. AEON. (2018m). Modesty is not a cranky killjoy but a way to get more from life. https://aeon.co/essays/modesty-is-not-a-cranky-killjoy-but-a-way-to-get-more-from-life

50. Aeon. (2018n). The globalisation of ideas will be different than that of goods. https://aeon.co/essays/the-globalisation-of-ideas-will-be-different-than-that-of-goods

51. Aeon. (2018o). How economists rode maths to become our era's astrologers. https://aeon.co/essays/how-economists-rode-maths-to-become-our-era-s-astrologers

52. Aeon. (2018p). Too much theory leads economists to bad predictions. https://aeon.co/ideas/too-much-theory-leads-economists-to-bad-predictions

53. Aeon. (2018q). The strange and turbulent global world of ant geopolitics. https://aeon.co/essays/the-strange-and-turbulent-global-world-of-ant-geopolitics

54. Aeon. (2018r). Machiavelli on the problem of our impure beginnings.

WORLD PEACE

https://aeon.co/essays/machiavelli-on-the-problem-of-our-impure-beginnings

55. Aeon. (2018s). Science in flux: Is a revolution brewing in evolutionary theory? https://aeon.co/essays/science-in-flux-is-a-revolution-brewing-in-evolutionary-theory

56. Aeon. (2018t). We should be wary about what big history overlooks in its myth. https://aeon.co/essays/we-should-be-wary-about-what-big-history-overlooks-in-its-myth

57. Aeon. (2018u). What should Econ 101 courses teach students today? https://aeon.co/essays/what-should-econ-101-courses-teach-students-today

58. Aeon. (2018v). How Georg Simmel diagnosed what makes city life distinctly modern. https://aeon.co/essays/how-georg-simmel-diagnosed-what-makes-city-life-distinctly-modern

59. Aeon. (2018w). Are plagues and wars the only ways to reduce inequality? https://aeon.co/essays/are-plagues-and-wars-the-only-ways-to-reduce-inequality

60. Aeon. (2018x). How Kerala went from poor to prosperous among India's states. https://aeon.co/essays/how-did-kerala-go-from-poor-to-prosperous-among-indias-states

61. Aeon. (2018y). Why everyone needs to learn some economics. https://aeon.co/essays/why-everyone-needs-to-learn-some-economics

62. Aeon. (2019a). How China remakes its cultural imports from the West. https://aeon.co/essays/how-china-remakes-its-cultural-imports-from-the-west

63. Aeon. (2019b). Why the utopian vision of William Morris is now within reach. https://aeon.co/essays/why-the-utopian-vision-of-william-morris-is-now-within-reach

64. Aeon. (2019c). Science is a public good in peril; here's how to fix it. https://aeon.co/essays/science-is-a-public-good-in-peril-heres-how-to-fix-it

65. Aeon. (2020a). The US is a failed state thanks to its system of government. https://aeon.co/ideas/the-us-is-a-failed-state-thanks-to-its-system-of-government

66. Aeon. (2020b). Global cooperation depends on the strength of local connections. https://aeon.co/ideas/global-cooperation-depends-on-the-strength-of-local-connections

67. Aeon. (2021). Even the Anthropocene is nature at work transforming itself. https://aeon.co/essays/even-the-anthropocene-is-nature-at-work-transforming-itself

68. Aeon. (n.d.). *To end patriarchy, woman must first seize power over herself.* https://aeon.co/classics/to-end-patriarchy-woman-must-first-seize-power-over-herself

69. Aeon. (n.d.). *What can Aristotle teach us about the routes to happiness.* https://aeon.co/essays/what-can-aristotle-teach-us-about-the-routes-to-happiness

70. Al-Ghamdi, N. A. (2021). Ideological representation of fear and hope in online newspaper reports on COVID-19 in Saudi Arabia. ScienceDirect. https://www.sciencedirect.com/science/article/pii/S2405844021009671

71. Aljazeera. (2017). Refugee aid dries up in Greece as media interest wanes. http://www.aljazeera.com/blogs/europe/2017/08/refugee-aid-dries-greece-media-interest-wanes-170801190706290.html

72. Aljazeera. (n.d.-a). Inside USA. http://www.aljazeera.com/programmes/insideusa/insideusa.html

WORLD PEACE

73. Aljazeera.   (n.d.-b).   Documentaries. http://www.aljazeera.com/documentaries/
74. American Psychological Association. (n.d.). Agentic state. *APA   Dictionary   of Psychology*. https://dictionary.apa.org/agentic-state

75. Asseraf, A. (2017). What's so New About News? Aeon. https://aeon.co/essays/news-has-never-been-pristine-always-entangled-in-time
76. Baraniuk, C. (2018). Would you care if this feature had been written by a robot? BBC News. http://www.bbc.com/news/business-42858174
77. Bastiat, F. (1850/2013). The Law. (FEE ed.). https://fee.org/media/14951/thelaw.pdf
78. BBC News. (2017). Azerbaijan 'operated secret $3bn secret slush fund'. http://www.bbc.com/news/world-europe-41156933
79. BBC News. (2017a). Indian Supreme Court in landmark   ruling   on   privacy. http://www.bbc.com/news/world-asia-india-41033954
80. BBC News. (2017b). Teenage brains 'not wired for high   stakes'. http://www.bbc.com/news/science-environment-42152392
81. BBC News. (2017b). What price would you put on a passport?   http://www.bbc.com/news/business-41013873
82. BBC News. (2017c). Wealthy San Francisco residents lose private street over tax bill. http://www.bbc.com/news/world-us-canada-40861145
83. BBC News. (2017c). White nationalist leader Matt Heimbach   defends   violence   at   rally. http://www.pbs.org/newshour/rundown/white-nationalist-leader-matt-heimbach-defends-violence-saturdays-rally-charlottesville/

WORLD PEACE

84. BBC News. (2017d). Cars for cheese: Why a free trade deal may not be free. http://www.bbc.com/news/business-40792654

85. BBC News. (2017d). Fake news: What's the best way to tame the beast? http://www.bbc.com/news/business-40575479

86. BBC News. (2017f). Science funding: Will 'picking winners' work? http://www.bbc.com/news/science-environment-41101892

87. BBC News. (2017g). 'Dodgy' greenhouse gas data threatens Paris accord. http://www.bbc.com/news/science-environment-40669449

88. BBC News. (2018). Italy political crisis hits financial markets. http://www.bbc.com/news/business-44287455

89. BBC News. (2018a). Controversial copyright law rejected by EU Parliament. https://www.bbc.com/news/technology-44712475

90. BBC News. (2018b). European Parliament backs copyright changes. https://www.bbc.com/news/technology-45495550

91. BBC. (2017). How a corporate mission can drive young workers away. http://www.bbc.com/capital/story/20170822-how-a-corporate-mission-can-drive-young-workers-away

92. BBC. (2017a). Bitcoin rebels risk 'currency trading chaos'. http://www.bbc.com/news/technology-40779767

93. BBC. (2017a). Greece's disappearing whistled language. http://www.bbc.com/travel/story/20170731-greeces-disappearing-whistled-language

94. BBC. (2017a). The case against personal brands. http://www.bbc.com/capital/story/20170723-the-case-against-personal-brands
95. BBC. (2017a, August 23). The Fijian villages that require approval to enter. https://www.bbc.com/travel/story/20170823-the-fijian-villages-that-require-approval-to-enter
96. BBC. (2017b). The ships that could change the seas forever. http://www.bbc.com/future/story/20170918-the-ships-that-could-change-the-seas-forever
97. BBC. (2017b). Wage squeeze to get tighter. http://www.bbc.com/news/business-40813256
98. BBC. (2017b, July 13). What will the challenges of 2050 be? *BBC Future*. http://www.bbc.com/future/story/20170713-what-will-the-challenges-of-2050-be
99. BBC. (2017c). A new man takes over the Fed: What will he do? http://www.bbc.com/news/42904545
100. BBC. (2017c). How business is driving the new space race. http://www.bbc.com/news/av/business-40940721/how-business-is-driving-the-new-space-race
101. BBC. (2017c). How plastic is slowly killing our sea creatures, fish and birds. http://www.bbc.co.uk/newsbeat/article/42030979/blue-planet-2-how-plastic-is-slowly-killing-our-sea-creatures-fish-and-birds
102. BBC. (2017d). An easy way to read more each year. http://www.bbc.com/capital/story/20170825-an-easy-way-to-read-more-each-year
103. BBC. (2017d). Tracking terrorists online might invade your privacy. http://www.bbc.com/future/story/20170808-

tracking-terrorists-online-might-invade-your-
privacy
104.BBC. (2017d). US deficit by year.
https://www.thebalance.com/us-deficit-by-year-
3306306
105.BBC. (2017e). Is this the next financial scandal
waiting to happen?
http://www.bbc.com/news/business-40704306
106.BBC. (2017e). Why video games are obsessed with
the apocalypse.
http://www.bbc.com/future/story/20170815-why-
video-games-are-obsessed-with-the-apocalypse
107.BBC. (2017e). World Europe.
http://www.bbc.com/news/world-europe-41314948
108.BBC. (2017f). Bitcoin CME futures.
http://money.cnn.com/2017/12/18/investing/bitcoin-
cme-futures/index.html
109.BBC. (2017f). News live.
http://www.bbc.com/news/live/world-41879690
110.BBC. (2017g). Blue Planet 2.
http://www.bbc.co.uk/newsbeat/article/42030979/bl
ue-planet-2-how-plastic-is-slowly-killing-our-sea-
creatures-fish-and-birds
111.BBC. (2017g). What's the economic impact of a
Korean conflict?
http://www.bbc.com/news/business-41495718
112.BBC. (2018). The country where Facebook posts
whipped up hate. https://www.bbc.com/news/blogs-
trending-45449938
113.BBC. (2018, July 5). Facebook finds independence
document
'racist'. https://www.bbc.com/news/technology-
44722728

114.BBC. (2018a). What it's like to live in a well-
governed country.

http://www.bbc.com/travel/story/20180107-what-its-like-to-live-in-a-well-governed-country

115.Bell, A. R., Brooks, C., & Moore, T. K. (2009). Interest in Medieval Accounts: Examples from England, 1272–1340. *History*, 94(4), 411-433. http://www.jstor.org/stable/24429091

116.Biello, D. (2009, January 2). Did a comet hit Earth 12,000 years ago? Scientific American. https://www.scientificamerican.com/article/did-a-comet-hit-earth-12900-years-ago/

117.Blacksmith Institute & Green Cross. (n.d.). The world's worst pollution problems: The top ten of the toxic twenty.

118.Bradford, A. (2017). Pollution facts & types of pollution. LiveScience. https://www.livescience.com/22728-pollution-facts.html

119.Brading, K. (2015). What Albert Einstein owes to David Hume's notion of time. *Aeon*. https://aeon.co/essays/what-albert-einstein-owes-to-david-humes-notion-of-time

120.Britannica. (2025). *Ideology: Nature, history, & significance*. https://www.britannica.com/topic/ideology-society

121.Britannica. (n.d.). Economic theory. https://www.britannica.com/topic/economic-theory

122.Britannica. (n.d.). Political economy. https://www.britannica.com/topic/political-economy

123.California Coastal Commission. (n.d.). Marine debris. State of California.

124.Chambers, N. B. (2011). How infrastructure makes water work for us. Palgrave Macmillan.

125.Charles, D. (2019, June 19). More bad buzz for bees: Record numbers of honey bee colonies died last winter. *NPR*.

WORLD PEACE

https://www.npr.org/sections/thesalt/2019/06/19/73
3761393/more-bad-buzz-for-bees-record-numbers-
of-honey-bee-colonies-died-last-winter
126.Chomsky, N. (2003). Rebel Without a Pause. [Film].
http://www.imdb.com/title/tt0368083/
127.CNN. (2017). Bitcoin does not protect against fraud.
https://therealnews.com/stories/bitcoin-does-not-
protect-against-fraud
128.CNN. (2017, June 28). Anti-media attacks on President
Trump. http://money.cnn.com/2017/06/28/media/anti-
media-attacks-president-trump/index.html

129.CNN. (2017a). HIV zero transmission prevention
vaccine   study.
http://www.cnn.com/2017/07/25/health/hiv-zero-
transmission-prevention-vaccine-study/index.html
130.CNN. (2017a). Hong Kong dolphins.
http://www.cnn.com/2017/09/21/asia/hong-kong-
dolphins/index.html
131.CNN. (2017a). Why so many people fall for scams.
http://www.bbc.com/capital/story/20180727-why-
so-many-people-fall-for-scams
132.CNN. (2017b). Famine coalition care.
http://www.cnn.com/2017/07/14/world/iyw-famine-
coalition-care/index.html
133.CNN. (2017b). Fatal traffic accidents.
http://money.cnn.com/2017/10/06/autos/fatal-
traffic-accidents/index.html
134.CNN. (2017b). Harvard affirmative action, Justice
Department.
http://www.cnn.com/2017/11/21/politics/harvard-
affirmative-action-justice-department/index.html
135.CNN. (2017c). Ancient population discovery
Alaska.
http://www.cnn.com/2018/01/05/health/ancient-
population-discovery-alaska-trnd/index.html

136.CNN. (2019, April 3). Facebook records exposed on Amazon servers. https://www.cnn.com/2019/04/03/tech/facebook -records-exposed-amazon/index.html

137.Compiler Press. (n.d.). *Ideological evolution.* http://www.compilerpress.ca/Competitiveness/Disse rtation%204/Synopsis%2006%2001.htm

138.Davidow, B. (2021). Programming human behavior at scale. LinkedIn. https://www.linkedin.com/pulse/programming-human-behavior-scale-the-technological-powering-davidow

139.EFF. (n.d.). Electronic Frontier Foundation. https://www.eff.org/

140.Estes, J. A., Dayton, P. K., Kareiva, P., Levin, S. A., Lubchenco, J., Menge, B. A., Palumbi, S. R., Power, M. E., & Terborgh, J. (2016). A keystone ecologist: Robert Treat Paine, 1933–2016. *Ecology, 97*(10), 2619–2624. https://doi.org/10.1002/ecy.1572

141.FEE. (2015). The Law by Frédéric Bastiat. https://fee.org/media/14951/thelaw.pdf

142.Fox News. (2019). No alien life in stars study. https://www.foxnews.com/science/no-alien-life-stars-study

143.Galer, S. S. (2017, July 7). The 24 best podcasts to make you smarter. *BBC Future.* http://www.bbc.com/future/story/20170707-the-24-best-podcasts-to-make-you-smarter

144.Gallagher, J. (2017, August 30). First cancer 'living drug' gets go-ahead. BBC News. http://www.bbc.com/news/health-41094990

145.Glaeser, E. L., & Scheinkman, J. (1998). Neither a Borrower Nor a Lender Be: An Economic Analysis of Interest Restrictions and Usury Laws. *The Journal*

WORLD PEACE

of Law & Economics, 41(1), 1-36. http://www.jstor.org/stable/10.1086/467383
146. GoodPlanet. (n.d.). http://www.goodplanet.org
147. Graeber, D. (2018). Bullshit Jobs: A Theory.
148. Grens, K. (2011). Air pollution tied to lung cancer in non-smokers. Thomas Reuters.
149. International Covenant on Economic, Social and Cultural Rights. (n.d.). In Wikipedia. https://en.wikipedia.org/wiki/International_Covenant_on_Economic,_Social_and_Cultural_Rights
150. Hemingway, M. (2021). Rigged: How the Media, Big Tech, and the Democrats Seized Our Elections. Regnery.
151. Hill, J. (2018). Nationalism in heart of Europe needles EU. https://www.bbc.co.uk/news/world-europe-43157234
152. ICIJ. (2018). Paradise Papers. https://www.icij.org/investigations/paradise-papers/
153. ICIJ. (2021). Pandora Papers. https://www.icij.org/investigations/pandora-papers/
154. ICIJ. (n.d.-a). Windfalls of war. https://www.icij.org/investigations/windfalls-war/
155. ICIJ. (n.d.-b). Making a killing. https://www.icij.org/investigations/makingkilling/
156. IEEE. (2004). The environmental impacts of electronics: Going beyond the walls of semiconductor fabs. *IEEE International Symposium on Electronics and the Environment, 2004. Conference Record*, 10–13 May 2004. https://ieeexplore.ieee.org/abstract/document/1299707/

157. IMDb. (n.d.). The Corporation. http://www.imdb.com/title/tt0379225/?ref_=fn_al_tt_1
158. Indystar. (2018). District court judge rules against pregnant woman mauled.

WORLD PEACE

https://www.indystar.com/story/news/crime/2018/1
0/02/district-court-judge-rules-against-pregnant-
woman-mauled-impd-k-9-2015/1499200002/

159. International Criminal Court. (n.d.). https://www.icc-cpi.int

160. Johannson-Stenman, O. (2018). We have an ethical obligation to relieve individual animal suffering. *Aeon*. https://aeon.co/ideas/we-have-an-ethical-obligation-to-relieve-individual-animal-suffering

161. Jolly, F. (2018). The world can learn from South Africa's ideal of nonracial democracy. *Aeon*. https://aeon.co/essays/the-world-can-learn-from-south-africas-ideal-of-nonracial-democracy

162. Joseph, P. (Director). (2007). Zeitgeist [Film]. https://www.imdb.com/title/tt1166827/

163. Joseph, P. (Director). (2008). Zeitgeist: Addendum [Film]. https://www.imdb.com/title/tt1332128/

164. Joseph, P. (Director). (2011). Zeitgeist: Moving Forward [Film]. https://www.imdb.com/title/tt1781069/

165. Lakatos, I. (1978). The methodology of scientific research programmes. Cambridge University Press.

166. Levine–King, R. (2018). Who Will the Retail Apocalypse Claim in 2018? BBC News. http://www.bbc.com/news/world-us-canada-42418902

167. LiveScience. (n.d.). Pollution facts. https://www.livescience.com/22728-pollution-facts.html

168. Lutz, W. D. (1989). *Doublespeak: From "Revenue Enhancement" to "Terminal Living"*. Harper & Row. https://en.wikipedia.org/wiki/William_D._Lutz

169. Military.com. (2020). Will coronavirus slow world's conflicts or intensify them? https://www.military.com/daily-

WORLD PEACE

news/2020/03/22/will-coronavirus-slow-worlds-conflicts-or-intensify-them.html
170.Mills, R. (2017). Why are countries laying claim to the deep-sea floor? BBC News. http://www.bbc.com/news/world-40248866
171.MSN. (2021b). Why did Homo sapiens emerge in Africa? https://www.msn.com/en-us/news/technology/why-did-homo-sapiens-emerge-in-africa/ar-BB1n4Fy7
172.MSN. (2023). A toe bone leads to my unified theory of Hindu mythology and anthropology. https://www.msn.com/en-us/news/world/a-toe-bone-leads-to-my-unified-theory-of-hindu-mythology-and-anthropology/ar-BB1i59Ts?ocid=entnewsntp&pc=DCTS

173.Murse, T. (2020). Politician salaries in the United States. ThoughtCo. https://www.thoughtco.com/how-much-do-politicians-earn-3367616
174.New York Times. (2006). The accidental invention of the Illuminati conspiracy. http://www.bbc.com/future/story/20170809-the-accidental-invention-of-the-illuminati-conspiracy
175.NPR. (2019). Is the Supreme Court going to soon give haters of the 'deep state' what they want? https://www.npr.org/2019/06/21/732178487/is-the-supreme-court-going-to-soon-give-haters-of-the-deep-state-what-they-want
176.NPR. (2020). Ghost DNA in West Africans complicates story of human origins. https://www.npr.org/2020/02/12/805237120/ghost-dna-in-west-africans-complicates-story-of-human-origins

177. NPTrust. (n.d.). Charitable giving statistics. https://www.nptrust.org/philanthropic-resources/charitable-giving-statistics
178. Numbeo. (n.d.). Pollution rankings by country. https://www.numbeo.com/pollution/rankings_by_co untry.jsp
179. OpenStax. (2023). Understanding bureaucracies and their types. In American Government 3e. https://socialsci.libretexts.org/Bookshelves/Political _Science_and_Civics/American_Government_3e_(OpenStax)/15%3A_The_Bureaucracy/15.04%3A_ Understanding_Bureaucracies_and_their_Types
180. ORNL. (n.d.). Genetic programming for understanding cognitive biases that generate polarization in social networks. https://www.ornl.gov/publication/genetic-programming-understanding-cognitive-biases-generate-polarization-social
181. Oxford Academic. (n.d.). 6 Rationality as a virtue. https://academic.oup.com/book/8196/chapter/15373 3961
182. Paradise Papers, BBC News. (2017, November 10). Everything you need to know about the leak. http://www.bbc.com/news/world-41880153
183. PBS. (2017). No one is coming: Hospice patients abandoned at death's door. https://www.pbs.org/newshour/health/no-one-is-coming-hospice-patients-abandoned-at-deaths-door
184. PBS. (2017a). Analysis: Women continue to make less than men. http://www.pbs.org/newshour/making-sense/analysis-women-continue-make-less-men/
185. PBS. (2017b). Teaching kids about Thanksgiving or Columbus? They deserve the real story. https://www.pbs.org/newshour/education/teaching

-kids-about-thanksgiving-or-columbus-they-deserve-the-real-story

186.Perera, A. (2017). Cows to planes: Indian ministers who rewrote scientific history. http://www.bbc.com/news/world-asia-india-41344136

187.Peter Bils. (2024). *Ideological infection.* http://peterbils.com/wp-content/uploads/2024/11/Crisis_Evolution-3.pdf

188.Peterson v. Sorlien, 299 N.W.2d 123, 127 (Minn. 1980), cert. denied, 450 U.S. 1031 (1981). https://kb.osu.edu/bitstreams/808226fc-d135-5165-ae37-786f84e5bd40/download

189.Planet Ocean. (2012). [Film]. Yann Arthus-Bertrand & Michael Pitiot (Directors). https://www.imdb.com/title/tt2240784/

190.Politifact. (2016). Inside fact-checking: How to decide what's true. http://www.politifact.com/truth-o-meter/article/2016/sep/14/inside-fact-checking-lucas-graves-author-deciding/

191.ProPublica. (2018). From ministry to muckraking: The biblical basis for investigative reporting. https://www.propublica.org/article/from-ministry-to-muckraking-the-biblical-basis-for-investigative-reporting

192.ProPublica. (2019). Natural gas industry beats a tiny West Virginia county. https://www.propublica.org/article/natural-gas-industry-beats-a-tiny-west-virginia-county

193.ProPublica. (n.d.). Course load: The growing burden of college fees. https://www.propublica.org/article/course-load-the-growing-burden-of-college-fees

194. ProPublica. (n.d.-a). Too broke for bankruptcy. https://www.propublica.org/series/too-broke-for-bankruptcy
195. ProPublica. (n.d.-b). Ignoring innocence. https://www.propublica.org/series/ignoring-innocence
196. Pulitzer Center. (n.d.). *No bars, no chains, no locks: How Finland is reimagining incarceration.* https://pulitzercenter.org/stories/no-bars-no-chains-no-locks-how-finland-reimagining-incarceration
197. Quora. (n.d.). Why is oil priced and traded in U.S. dollars? https://www.quora.com/Why-is-oil-priced-and-traded-in-U-S-dollars?share=1
198. Reclaim Democracy. (n.d.-a). Arbitration: Justice denied? http://reclaimdemocracy.org/arbitration-justice-denied/
199. Reclaim Democracy. (n.d.-a). Corporate personhood. http://reclaimdemocracy.org/corporate-personhood/
200. Reclaim Democracy. (n.d.-b). US presidential debates: Parties, corporations. http://reclaimdemocracy.org/us-presidential-debates-parties-corporations/
201. Robinson, B. H. (2009). E-waste: An assessment of global production and environmental impacts. Science of The Total Environment, 408(2), 183-191. https://www.sciencedirect.com/science/article/pii/S0048969709009073
202. Rome Statute of the International Criminal Court. (1998). https://www.icc-cpi.int/nr/rdonlyres/ea9aeff7-5752-4f84-be94-0a655eb30e16/0/rome_statute_english.pdf
203. Rose, N. (2020). The triage of truth: Do not take expert opinion lying down. *Aeon.* https://aeon.co/ideas/the-triage-of-truth-do-not-take-expert-opinion-lying-down

WORLD PEACE

204.Savage, M. (2017). Why Sweden is close to becoming a cashless economy. BBC News. http://www.bbc.com/news/business-41095004
205.Schmitz, R. (2019, June 19). Nearly 71 million people forcibly displaced worldwide in 2018, says U.N. report. *NPR*. https://www.npr.org/2019/06/19/733945696/nearly-71-million-people-forcibly-displaced-worldwide-in-2018-says-u-n-report
206.Science Daily. (2008, January 7). Big pharma spends more on advertising than research and development, study finds. https://www.sciencedaily.com/releases/2008/01/080105140107.htm
207.ScienceDaily. (2007). https://www.sciencedaily.com/releases/2007/08/070813162438.htm
208.SCU. (n.d.). Journalism Ethics Resources: Trust in journalism—A bibliography. https://www.scu.edu/ethics/focus-areas/journalism-ethics/resources/trust-in-journalism-a-bibliography/
209.Seltzer, L. F. (2012, October 17). Greed: The ultimate addiction. *Psychology Today*. https://www.psychologytoday.com/us/blog/evolution-the-self/201210/greed-the-ultimate-addiction
210.Smithsonian Magazine. (2020). DNA suggests modern humans emerged from several groups in Africa, not one. https://www.smithsonianmag.com/smart-news/dna-suggests-modern-humans-emerged-from-several-groups-in-africa-not-one-180982242/
211.Sng, T.-H., & Moriguchi, C. (2014). Like the emperor's new clothes: DNA kits are tailored for the vain. AEON. https://aeon.co/ideas/like-the-

WORLD PEACE

emperors-new-clothes-dna-kits-are-tailored-for-the-vain
212.SocialSci LibreTexts. (2023). Understanding bureaucracies and their types. https://socialsci.libretexts.org/Bookshelves/Political _Science_and_Civics/American_Government_3e_(OpenStax)/15%3A_The_Bureaucracy/15.04%3A_ Understanding_Bureaucracies_and_their_Types
213.Solman, P. (2017, July 20). How do we invest in the future of humanity? Swedish philosopher Nick Bostrom explains. *PBS NewsHour*. http://www.pbs.org/newshour/making-sense/invest-future-humanity-swedish-philosopher-nick-bostrom-explains/

214.Statista. (n.d.). Marketing budgets of US health care companies. https://www.statista.com/statistics/275384/marketin g-budgets-of-us-health-care-companies/
215.Storrs, L. (2018). Aadhaar: India top court upholds world's largest biometric scheme. BBC News. https://www.bbc.com/news/world-asia-india-44777787
216.Streeck, W. (2017). How Will Capitalism End: Essays on a Failing System. Verso.
217.Street, M. (2018). The history of riot shows the importance of democratic tumult. *Aeon*. https://aeon.co/essays/the-history-of-riot-shows-the-importance-of-democratic-tumult

218.Sundaram, J. K. (2009a). Globalization, a "devastating success". https://therealnews.com/stories/jomokwame0911pt1
219.Sussman, R. (2019). Human dignity is an ideal with remarkably shallow

roots. *Aeon*. https://aeon.co/essays/human-dignity-is-an-ideal-with-remarkably-shallow-roots

220. Szasz, T. S. (1973). Ideology and insanity. *International Social Science Journal*, 25(4), 504–511. https://unesdoc.unesco.org/ark:/48223/pf0000007128

221. Tasioulas, J. (2017). Are human rights anything more than legal conventions? Aeon. https://aeon.co/ideas/are-human-rights-anything-more-than-legal-conventions

222. The Age of Consequences. (2016). [Film]. Jared P. Scott (Director). http://www.imdb.com/title/tt5098712/?ref_=nv_sr_1

223. The Conversation. (2018). It's getting harder to prosecute politicians for corruption. https://theconversation.com/its-getting-harder-to-prosecute-politicians-for-corruption-91609

224. The Corporation. (n.d.). http://thecorporation.com/

225. The Real News. (2017a). Average CEO makes 339 times more than their average worker. https://therealnews.com/stories/average-ceo-makes-339-times-more-than-their-average-worker

226. The Real News. (2019). Baltimore mayor signs charter amendment banning water privatization. https://therealnews.com/columns/baltimore-mayor-signs-charter-amendment-banning-water-privatization

227. Therealnews. (n.d.-a). Merchants of death: How the military-industrial complex profits from endless war. https://therealnews.com/stories/merchants-of-death-how-the-military-industrial-complex-profits-from-endless-war

WORLD PEACE

228.Therealnews. (n.d.-a). Stop the fast track to a future of global corporate rule. https://therealnews.com/columns/stop-the-fast-track-to-a-future-of-global-corporate-rule

229.Therealnews. (n.d.-b). Space Force: $716B defense bill take wasteful military spending to new heights. https://therealnews.com/stories/space-force-716b-defense-bill-take-wasteful-military-spending-to-new-heights

230.Therealnews. (n.d.-c). Economic update: Hidden failures of capitalism. https://therealnews.com/stories/economic-update-hidden-failures-of-capitalism

231.Thomas, D. (2017, August 16). How to turn a hit TV show into an international success. *BBC News*. http://www.bbc.com/news/business-40301134

232.Time. (2013). Rare earths are too rare. http://science.time.com/2013/12/20/rare-earths-are-too-rare/

233.TRNN. (2018a). Supreme Court rules in favor of big business, limits workers' rights to trials. https://therealnews.com/stories/supreme-court-rules-in-favor-of-big-business-limits-workers-rights-to-trials

234.TRNN. (2018b). Congress passes bank lobbyists bill. https://therealnews.com/stories/congress-passes-bank-lobbyists-bill-an-unnecessary-giveaway-to-banks

235.TRNN. (2018c). Debunking John Oliver on Venezuela. https://therealnews.com/stories/debunking-john-oliver-on-venezuela

236.TRNN. (2018d). Global capitalism: Linking Trump and Marx's critique of capitalism.

https://therealnews.com/stories/global-capitalism-linking-trump-and-marxs-critique-of-capitalism

237. U.S. EPA. (n.d.-a). Nonpoint source pollution: The nation's largest water quality problem.

238. U.S. EPA. (n.d.-b). Non-hazardous waste | Basic information.

239. UNICEF. (2017). Babies' brains damaged by pollution, UNICEF says. http://www.bbc.com/news/health-42250558

240. United Nations Environment Program. (n.d.). Marine litter: Trash that kills.

241. Wake Forest University. (2020). State governments and power during the pandemic. https://news.wfu.edu/2020/05/28/state-governments-and-power-during-the-pandemic/

242. Wakefield, J. (2018). Google tracks users who turn off location history. BBC News. https://www.bbc.com/news/technology-45183041

243. Washington Post. (2015). Big pharmaceutical companies are spending far more on marketing than research. https://www.washingtonpost.com/news/wonk/wp/2015/02/11/big-pharmaceutical-companies-are-spending-far-more-on-marketing-than-research/?noredirect=on&utm_term=.0e25605e681d

244. Wikipedia. (n.d.). *Deprogramming.* https://en.wikipedia.org/wiki/Deprogramming

245. Wikipedia. (n.d.). *Ideology.* https://en.wikipedia.org/wiki/Ideology

246. Wikipedia. (n.d.-a). Bureaucracy. https://en.wikipedia.org/wiki/Bureaucracy

247. Wikipedia. (n.d.a). De-banking. https://en.wikipedia.org/wiki/De-banking

WORLD PEACE

248. Wikipedia. (n.d.-a). Government. https://en.wikipedia.org/wiki/Government

249. Wikipedia. (n.d.-a). History of capitalist theory. https://en.wikipedia.org/wiki/History_of_capitalist_theory

250. Wikipedia. (n.d.-a). History of insurance. https://en.wikipedia.org/wiki/History_of_insurance

251. Wikipedia. (n.d.-a). Joint-stock company—Early joint-stock companies. https://en.wikipedia.org/wiki/Joint-stock_company#Early_joint-stock_companies

252. Wikipedia. (n.d.-a). Mafia (party game). https://en.wikipedia.org/wiki/Mafia_(party_game)

253. Wikipedia. (n.d.-b). International Covenant on Economic, Social and Cultural Rights. https://en.wikipedia.org/wiki/International_Covenant_on_Economic,_Social_and_Cultural_Rights

254. Wikipedia. (n.d.-b). List of oldest companies. https://en.wikipedia.org/wiki/List_of_oldest_companies

255. Wikipedia. (n.d.-b). Philip Converse. https://en.wikipedia.org/wiki/Philip_Converse

256. Wikipedia. (n.d.-b). Poor People's Campaign: A National Call for a Moral Revival. https://en.wikipedia.org/wiki/Poor_People's_Campaign:_A_National_Call_for_a_Moral_Revival

257. Wikipedia. (n.d.-b). Sovereign immunity in the United States. https://en.wikipedia.org/wiki/Sovereign_immunity_in_the_United_States

258. Wikipedia. (n.d.-b). Tulip mania. https://en.wikipedia.org/wiki/Tulip_mania

259. Wikipedia. (n.d.-c). Foreign Sovereign Immunities Act. https://en.wikipedia.org/wiki/Foreign_Sovereign_Immunities_Act

WORLD PEACE

260. Wikipedia. (n.d.-c). List of ongoing armed conflicts. https://en.wikipedia.org/wiki/List_of_ongoing_arme d_conflicts

261. Wikipedia. (n.d.-c). Malum in se. https://en.wikipedia.org/wiki/Malum_in_se

262. Wikipedia. (n.d.c). Panama Papers. https://en.wikipedia.org/wiki/Panama_Papers

263. Wikipedia. (n.d.-d). Ideology. https://en.wikipedia.org/wiki/Ideology

264. Wikipedia. (n.d.-d). William D. Lutz. https://en.wikipedia.org/wiki/William_D._Lutz

265. Wikipedia. (n.d.-e). Health insurance in the United States. https://en.wikipedia.org/wiki/Health_insurance_in_t he_United_States

266. Wikipedia. (n.d.-f). Jaywalking. https://en.wikipedia.org/wiki/Jaywalking

267. Wikipedia. (n.d.-g). Economic ideology. https://en.wikipedia.org/wiki/Economic_ideology

268. Wikiquote. (n.d.). Frédéric Bastiat. https://en.wikiquote.org/wiki/Fr%C3%A9d%C3%A 9ric_Bastiat

269. World Bank. (2024). March 2024 global poverty update. https://blogs.worldbank.org/en/opendata/march-2024-global-poverty-update-from-the-world-bank--first-esti

270. World Happiness Report. (2018). http://worldhappiness.report/ed/2018/

271. World Health Organization. (2014). Climate change and health.

272. Worldwatch Institute. (n.d.). The state of consumption today.

273. Yale. (2017). Boom in mining rare earths poses mounting toxic risks. http://e360.yale.edu/features/boom_in_mining_rare _earths_poses_mounting_toxic_risks

274. Yeston, J., Coontz, R., Smith, J., & Ash, C. (2006). A thirsty world. Science, 313(5790), 1067. http://science.sciencemag.org/content/313/5790/106 7

275. Zmigrod, L. (2021). A neurocognitive model of ideological thinking. Cambridge University. https://www.cambridge.org/core/services/aop-cambridge-core/content/view/38CBDADC3414FA5783AE273 0FAF36ACD/S0730938421000101a.pdf/neurocogn itive_model_of_ideological_thinking.pdf

276. Zmigrod, L. (2021). A psychology of ideology: Unpacking the psychological structure of ideological thinking. *Perspectives on Psychological Science*, 17(4), 915–936. https://doi.org/10.1177/17456916211044140

277. Zuboff, S. (2019). The Age of Surveillance Capitalism. PublicAffairs.